Rusty, Marcia
and Marcia

May God continue his Blessing
upon you.

May the B.Ble continue
to inspire you.

Your Friend,

Mike Mc Intosh

FALLING
IN LOVE WITH
THE BIBLE

FALLING
IN LOVE WITH
THE BIBLE

by Mike MacIntosh

Victor®
The Bible Teacher's Teacher

COOK COMMUNICATIONS MINISTRIES
Colorado Springs, Colorado • Paris, Ontario
KINGSWAY COMMUNICATIONS LTD
Eastbourne, England

Victor® is an imprint of Cook Communications Ministries,
Colorado Springs, CO 80918
Cook Communications, Paris, Ontario
Kingsway Communications, Eastbourne, England

FALLING IN LOVE WITH THE BIBLE
© 2005 by Mike MacIntosh

Cover Design, Greg Jackson/JacksonDesignCo.llc
© Photo by Joe Matisek

First Printing, 2005
Printed in the United States of America
1 2 3 4 5 6 7 8 9 10 Printing/Year 09 08 07 06 05

ISBN: 0781441366

Library of Congress Cataloging-in-Publication Data

MacIntosh, Mike, 1944-
  Falling in love with the Bible / Mike MacIntosh.
    p. cm.
  Includes bibliographical references.
  ISBN 0-7814-4136-6
  1. Bible--Reading. I. Title.
  BS617.M26 2005
  220--dc22
                            2004029411

I dedicate this book to my pastor, Chuck Smith. When I became a Christian at the age of twenty-six, it was after several years of seeking God through gurus, mysticism, and Eastern religion and philosophies and every pop idea that the 1960s had to offer. It seems I had been tricked and deceived by the Devil all of my life. When I found myself listening to a Bible study, I was challenged with the truth. After I had made a commitment to God, I said a simple prayer to God, "Please lead me to someone who will teach me the Bible—not someone who will try to be my guru or make me join an organization."

Within a couple of weeks, I was attending every Bible study Chuck taught. Chuck has fulfilled my prayer by always pointing me toward Jesus and encouraging my independence by being dependent upon God. I can never thank Chuck enough for teaching me to fall in love with the Bible.

Jesus said, "The student is not greater than the teacher, nor the servant than the master." Like a really good teacher, Chuck taught me to be God's disciple, not his disciple. Chuck taught me to follow Jesus, not to follow him. Chuck taught me to put all of my trust in the Bible and live by its tenets.

I can never say thank you enough to the Lord for putting such a humble and spiritual teacher into my life. He has never let me down because he always points me to God.

CONTENTS

ACKNOWLEDGMENTS

I am thankful for the dedicated people at Cook Communications and their commitment to the Gospel.

Thanks to my editor, Keith Wall, for his perseverance with my busy schedule. He is teachable and a good teacher.

Thanks to all of the wonderful people who pray for me and love me. It makes writing a joy for me. I see them in my mind's eye as the audience who will continue to lead others to Jesus. And it is for them that I write the encouraging words of this book.

Special thanks to Sandy, my wife, who always stands with me and always prays for me and is always in love with the Bible.

I would like to acknowledge the work of the Holy Spirit, which is always fresh and encouraging during a project like *Falling in Love with the Bible.*

WHEN YOU OPEN THE BIBLE, EXPECT A MIRACLE

The writer Robert Zend once quipped, "People throughout the world have one thing in common: They're all different." It is true that people are different; however, all of us share certain things in common as well. We all are seeking purpose and meaning in life. We want to know the answer to the question that has haunted philosophers for eons: "Why am I here? I know that I exist, but *why* do I exist?"

I have been in the ministry for over fifty years and have spoken to thousands of people—young and old, rich and poor. The question I hear most often is either "What's the secret of a successful life?" or "How can I have an effective ministry?" My answer is always the same: "There is no secret to it. If you want your life to be full and meaningful, become intimately acquainted with God, the God who desires a meaningful relationship with you. The best way to develop this relationship is by knowing Him, and the only way to truly know Him is to read His revelation of Himself in the Bible. Read the Bible with an open mind and let it speak to you."

It seems incredible, but it is true—the Creator of this universe loves you and desires to reveal to you the purpose of your existence. This is the reason I encourage you to carefully read the book you are now holding, for Mike MacIntosh challenges you to take a fresh look at the Scriptures and to see how they pulsate with power. Mike assures us that as we fall in love with the Bible, we are certain to fall in love with its Author. As this happens, we are well on our way to discovering the purpose for our existence.

Mike doesn't just talk about the power of God's Word—he is a living example of how the Bible can dramatically change a person's life. When I first met Mike in 1970, he was in his early twenties. He had spent several years in a desperate search for meaning, but his wandering only brought him more confusion and frustration. When Mike first came to Calvary Chapel, he had an insatiable thirst for the Word of God. He attended every Bible study and drank in the Word. Mike discovered the truth of God's Word and put his trust in Jesus Christ. We watched the miracles of God's grace in Mike's life as the Lord completely transformed him. God changed Mike from a confused and dazed young man to a dynamic minister of Jesus Christ whose ministry has had an impact on the whole world.

What God did for Mike He desires to do for you, too. He is able to make minor changes or major overhauls in your life. No matter where you are in your journey, the encouragement and guidance Mike brings in these pages will point you in the right direction. Whether you need strength for the road ahead or clarity in understanding God's plan for the future, this book offers help and insights to propel you on your way. I am certain that *Falling in Love with the Bible* will motivate you to dig deeper into God's Word. And when you do, prepare for life-changing miracles.

—Chuck Smith
Costa Mesa, California

THE MOMENT I FELL IN LOVE

The year was 1966. The Beatles, flower power, miniskirts, the Ford Mustang, the Vietnam War, the Civil Rights movement, flag burnings, and a myriad of other icons were shaping the identity of the largest group of young Americans in the nation's history. Protests were held regularly, drugs were used rampantly, and traditions were challenged routinely. During that year of cultural convulsions, I was hanging out in Southern California, a time and a place where anything could happen—and usually did.

In the spring of '66, Southern California was saturated with so much sunshine that the region could have exported it to the other forty-nine states and made a profit. Born and raised for twenty-one years in drizzly, overcast Portland, Oregon, I bubbled over with joy to be surfing and tanning at Newport Beach in January and February.

Away from the depressing northwestern gloom, I felt as if life was unfolding at a wonderful pace. Electricity charged the air among the young people who were no longer in high school or living with their parents. We were a free and liberated generation heading nowhere fast. But it was an exhilarating time for our age group, because not only were we changing, but our culture was also radically transforming as well. The mores of our society were shifting dramatically. We heard songs and speeches assuring us

IF YOU FALL
IN LOVE WITH
THE BIBLE,
YOUR LIFE
WILL NEVER
BE THE SAME.

that a new day was dawning, a new era was unfolding with young people serving as the vanguard.

Looking back now, it is easy to see that we were in the midst of a cultural revolution. The United States of America that we were taught about from our first day in elementary school until graduation from college was no longer to be.

I can visualize those times so vividly in my mind's eye that as I write these words, I see the shimmering sunshine and the curling ocean waves as surfers ride them toward shore. One of the reasons these are such fond memories is that the scenery of that delightful '66 spring season served as the backdrop for a great romance. That's when I fell in love with a gorgeous young lady named Sandy.

We first met briefly as I arrived at her apartment to pick up one of her college girlfriends for a date. A couple of days later, I was back again as a guest at her birthday party. In less than a month, Sandy and I were standing before a justice of the peace in Las Vegas, Nevada, exchanging our marriage vows.

"Boy! That was fast!" you might say. We admit it was very fast, and it was also very romantic.

I knew she was the person for me, and she fell in love with me, too. It all clicked; it was meant to be. Or so it seemed. Never mind that we divorced two years later, only to remarry after another two-and-a-half years and stay married to this day (more on that in a moment). My point is that when I saw a good thing that I knew I wanted, I committed myself to it wholeheartedly.

That is exactly how another romance began—with the same kind of ardent enthusiasm and passion. I fell in love with the Bible. I knew it was a good thing and that it would help me grow as a spiritual man. My diet of the Scriptures began after the tumultuous loss of my marriage and of my mind—because like many other young people enjoying newfound freedoms of the sixties, I experimented with the evils of the day—which, like millions in our generation, caused me all kinds of problems.

> IF YOU WANT TO HAVE A GREAT LIFE—ONE FILLED WITH MEANING AND RICHNESS—IMMERSE YOURSELF IN THE SCRIPTURES.

It was through the power of the Holy Spirit that God worked to restore my life and my marriage. Being extremely wary of organized religion, I was not looking for a guru or some mystic to teach me. It was God who knew my need and made sure the Bible was exciting and challenging to me. Above all, He made it relevant to me when and where I needed it most. Each day as I sat down to read the Bible a little bit at a time, a sense of peace would sweep over me. I could sense the presence of heaven working within me.

It was one of those postcard-perfect summer days in Southern California, and I was sitting on a lawn chair in Huntington Beach. A friend of mine managed the Wind and Sea Surfboard Shop on the Pacific Coast Highway. I forgot about the traffic, the surfers at the Huntington Pier, the surf bunnies coming into the shop for tanning lotion and bikinis. The whole sun-and-surf scene was swirling around me, but I couldn't be bothered. My eyes were riveted to the pages of Holy Scripture. I was reading the Gospel According to Saint Luke. Every word, page by page, became illuminated to me. It was stunning to my mind and overwhelming to my being.

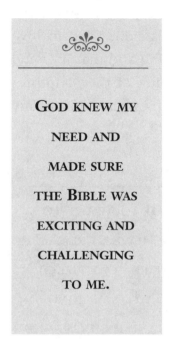

GOD KNEW MY NEED AND MADE SURE THE BIBLE WAS EXCITING AND CHALLENGING TO ME.

I remember reading the opening chapters of Luke and telling myself, *I have just read the Christmas story—the real Christmas story.* I could not believe it. The most famous story on earth is found in the Bible. And it filled in a lot of gaps from my childhood. This Holy Book, God's Word to mankind, said nothing about Christmas trees with tinsel or packages under the tree. There was nothing about Santa Claus and flying reindeer. Not one mention of mistletoe, egg nog, or front yards decorated with lights and snowmen. No, the Bible's version of the Christmas story featured a celebration of a much different kind than I was used to: It focused on the birth of a baby boy born to a poor carpenter named Joseph and a young Jewish girl named Mary. They could not find a motel room in the middle of the night. They actually gave birth in a stable filled with animals. That was all news to me!

I don't know if my words can express to you how I felt. We've all had that "light bulb" experience, when suddenly we get it. Our minds are abruptly and amazingly opened to new truths or insights. Well, I had light bulbs going off in my head like camera flashbulbs popping at the Super Bowl.

I read story after story, and somehow I instinctively knew that each one was absolutely true. These were not Sunday school tales to help kids be "good little boys and girls." It was the truth—life-changing truth. From that day forward, I was hooked on reading the Bible. I fell in love with the Bible just as I did with Sandy. And falling in love with the Bible drew me to fall in love with God. Even as the Beatles were singing, "You say you want a revolution," I was undergoing one of my own—a revolution of my heart, soul, and mind.

My life changed so radically for the better that after only a few months of daily reading, Sandy could see how different I had become. She also gave her heart to the Lord, and we were remarried after more than two years of divorce. After thirty-four years (the second time)—and five kids and fifteen grandkids—we are still married. And still in love. There's no doubt the wonderful life we've shared is because of our mutual love for God and His Word, which has guided us all along the way.

Here's what I want to say to you at the outset of this book: If you want to have a great life—one filled with meaning and richness—immerse yourself in the Scriptures. I commend the following pages to you, not as a theological workbook or a boring text on the Book I am pointing you to. But I commend the simple truths and genuine love described in the Scriptures. I commend to you the lifestyle that is laid out for you, and I recommend to you the God of all creation who inspired the Bible to be written.

If you fall in love with the Bible, your life will never be the same. It will be infinitely better, healthier, more satisfying. For when we fall in love with the Bible, we will inevitably fall in love with God Himself. And as He has promised, He is eager to bestow all good things on those who love Him and seek Him. Just as the psalmist wrote, "For the LORD God is a sun and shield; the LORD will give grace and glory; no good thing will he withhold from those who walk uprightly" (Psalm 84:11 NKJV). This is the same God who wants to speak to us, directly and intimately, through the words He inspired—the words that can change our lives in every way.

—MIKE MACINTOSH

CHAPTER ONE

COMMUNICATING WITH THE CREATOR

IF YOU FALL IN LOVE WITH THE BIBLE,
YOU'LL FALL IN LOVE WITH GOD

I believe the Bible is the best gift God has given to man.
ABRAHAM LINCOLN

I sat face-to-face with a man who had a five-inch scar running down his left cheek from ear to chin. The cut, gouged into his flesh by the butt of an army rifle, had never been stitched closed, nor had it ever been given medical attention. The result was an unsightly scar to say the least. But often it is the scars—either physical ones or emotional ones—that serve as reminders of what really matters in life.

It was 1976—six years after I first discovered the power of God's Word—and I sat on the floor across from this man in a thatched-roof hut in the jungles of what was then known as

Burma. Only a small, low table separated us. The one-room house where we gathered—which was built on stilts above the ground—had twenty-five other people jammed inside. Most of them were relatives who had come to meet this special family member, whose personal faith and courage seemed to stand as tall as Mount Everest. As I would soon find out, Jonathan Chan was an amazing person, a man with a love for God that oozed from the pores of his skin.

> THE BIBLE IS NOT A MUSTY OLD HISTORICAL BOOK FOR AGED MEN TO ANALYZE. IT IS A BOOK EVERYONE CAN ENJOY AND LEARN FROM.

Jonathan had traveled for two weeks through dangerous mountains and jungles just to meet with us and make arrangements to distribute Bibles. He would take thousands of copies, even tens of thousands, if our ministry team could provide them.

We had been told that Jonathan wanted to give Bibles to the people of his country on the border of Burma. But it was a perilous mission. The government had banned the Bible and made it a crime punishable by imprisonment to preach, evangelize, or distribute Christian material of any kind. This law, I would soon learn, was the reason this man bore the nasty scar on his face.

Jonathan was a preacher of the Scriptures, and he had traveled far and wide telling people about God's love. He knew the laws of his country forbade him to speak openly about God and

Jesus, but he believed his allegiance to the King of kings trumped earthly rules and decrees. He had a higher authority to answer to. Eventually, he was arrested and thrown into prison.

Being jailed did little to silence the man, so great was his faith that God's Word was the true source of freedom. He began telling fellow inmates about the God of the Bible, and many accepted God's redeeming love. Even the prison guards would listen to him expound from the stories of the Bible, and some of them, too, made commitments of faith.

After a few months of moving Jonathan from one cellblock to another, from one prison to another, the authorities made him an offer. It was a plea bargain of sorts. He could go free if he would only stop preaching and renounce his faith in God. If he would publicly proclaim that his stories about Jesus were bogus, he could be a free man.

One morning, authorities took Jonathan to the village square of his hometown, stood him up on a box, and positioned armed soldiers around him. There, he was given his opportunity: Denounce the Bible, and tell the gathering of people—including neighbors, family, and friends—that Jesus was not God's Son, nor was the Bible "God's book," nor was it true and accurate. He would then be released on his word that he would never again try to promote the Bible.

If he complied with those conditions, he would be free to rejoin his family and move on with his life. When his hands were loosed from the ropes that bound him, however, he told the people boldly that the Bible is indeed the Book of Truth and that it declares the wonderful story about the Creator of all things. He proclaimed that this God sent His only begotten Son, Jesus, to die on a cross for our sins.

21

This humble and soft-spoken man told me what happened next. "It was at this moment in my brief sermon that the soldiers threw me to the ground and beat me with their rifles," he said.

As the crowd stood stunned at the demonstration of brute force, the military personnel issued a gruff threat to everyone present and then left the area. Jonathan's limp body lay broken and motionless on the damp ground. Frustrated with dealing with this relentless man of faith, the authorities gave up and left him for dead.

Little did I know that my meeting with Jonathan would have a major impact on the rest of my life. Without a doubt, my pastor, Chuck Smith, had instilled in my heart a great appreciation for the Bible. But Jonathan had demonstrated to me the concept of devotion and commitment to the Bible—at all costs. This man truly loved the Bible, and I would leave our jungle encounter and walk the busy streets of San Diego with a new view of life and faith. The citizens of "America's Finest City" would be encouraged for the rest of my life to read the Bible and to discover God's greatness on every page.

> THE BIBLE IS NOT PAPER, INK, AND BINDING—IT IS POWER, STRENGTH, AND TRUTH.

Jonathan's story has been etched in the depths of my soul for three decades now. Even though I have met thousands of Christian men and women from dozens of countries over the years, his story has remained vivid in my mind. There was something very special to learn from this particular man.

This humble man of faith was willing to endure suffering,

imprisonment, beatings, and even death for one simple yet powerful truth: God's Word is the expression, the representation, and the articulation of God Himself. The Bible is not paper, ink, and binding—it is power, strength, and truth. It has a life of its own. And when its truths become real for the reader, the Bible's power transforms even the hardest skeptic.

There is a supernatural component to the Bible that elevates it far above the millions of other books written and published through the centuries. The writer of Hebrews tells us that "the word of God is living and active. Sharper than any double-edged sword, it penetrates even to dividing soul and spirit, joints and marrow; it judges the thoughts and attitudes of the heart" (4:12). We may read other books that are exciting or insightful or helpful—but only the Bible is the Holy Spirit-inspired, life-giving, joy-producing revelation from heaven. That is why people dedicate themselves, even under perilous circumstances, to preaching and teaching the Bible. It has the power to change everything about our earthly lives and our eternal destination.

GOD REVEALS HIMSELF TO US

The Christian faith can seem so mysterious, so incomprehensible. After all, to many people God is a "far out" concept. Who is He? Where did He come from? How can we possibly know this Supreme Being who lives way "up there"? If we can't see God or touch Him, how do we know He's really with us?

For most of my life I wrestled with these very issues. From an early age I questioned things about God. I remember hearing Bible stories when I was four years old that stimulated my young mind to question matters of life and faith. I would look out my bedroom window in the morning and see the sun's rays breaking through Portland's ever-present clouds, and I'd think that they were stairways for angels to come to the earth.

As a teenager in science class at school, I would look through the microscope at all those infinitesimal organisms and think, *Someone had to have created all this.* I can't believe the world with all its creatures and systems came about by an explosion. At home, I would watch TV shows about our universe and distant galaxies. I'd wonder if there was a God out there keeping the planets spinning.

Of course, it isn't only children who ponder the great mysteries of creation and the Creator. Throughout the ages, men and women—educated and uneducated, scholars and simpletons—have been trying to understand God. Indeed, humankind's ideas about God and "gods" are found in mythology and archeological discoveries that date back thousands of years.

But there is one major source of literature on old planet earth that gives us a clear understanding of God, along with a clear understanding of creation and its purpose. That source is the Holy Bible. The more you read it, the more you understand yourself, the world you live in, and the One who made both.

Saint Paul wrote in the first century to a young student of his the following words:

> *And without controversy great is the mystery of godliness: God was manifest in the flesh, justified in the Spirit, seen of angels, preached unto the Gentiles, believed on in the world, received up into glory (1 Timothy 3:16 KJV).*

He puts it succinctly, doesn't he? Godliness is a mystery, and mankind, with all of its worldly frustrations, has formed and shaped a myriad of religions and spiritual disciplines to try to uncover the truth about God. Listen carefully to me, please: With just a modicum of detective work you can easily understand this best-selling book of all time. Yes, it is true that throughout the ages people have built shrines and cathedrals and monuments to the God of the Bible. I am not sure He has asked for all of that. Yes, it is also true that throughout the ages people have designed religious schools and training centers for disciples of many cults, sects, religions, denominations, and beliefs.

THE MORE YOU READ THE BIBLE, THE MORE YOU UNDERSTAND YOURSELF, THE WORLD YOU LIVE IN, AND THE ONE WHO MADE BOTH.

Sometimes all of these institutions and rituals can make us feel more intimidated about reading the Bible. For instance, when the Midnight Mass is celebrated in Rome on Christmas Eve, people from just about every country in the world watch via television. The ceremony is full of ritual and tradition. Last time I watched this event on TV, it dawned on me that the church probably scares away many people. What I mean is that the liturgy of the cathedral is a bit overwhelming. The candles and the incense mixed with chanting and Latin words can overpower a person who is from a humble background. How in the world can you or I ever interpret the Holy Bible? After all, ministers have gone to college, graduate school, and seminary; they have studied Greek and

Hebrew. These are learned and wise people talking about the Bible!

The church can make the Bible appear to be a very sacred and holy book that only certain people can read, let alone interpret and understand. That is really sad to think about, but without doubt the church at large has failed to encourage and enable people to understand the Holy Scriptures. The Bible is not a musty old historical book for aged men to analyze. It is a book everyone can enjoy and learn from.

> IT HAS THE POWER TO CHANGE EVERYTHING ABOUT OUR EARTHLY LIVES AND OUR ETERNAL DESTINATION.

The Old Testament prophet Daniel said this about God: "He reveals deep and hidden things; he knows what lies in darkness, and light dwells with him. ... There is a God in heaven who reveals mysteries" (2:22, 28). We may at times struggle to grasp the complexities and enigmas of the faith, but the Lord discloses all we need to know in order to grow and prosper spiritually.

In the New Testament we are told that "All scripture is given by inspiration of God, and is profitable for doctrine, for reproof, for correction, for instruction in righteousness: That the man of God may be perfect, thoroughly furnished unto all good works" (2 Timothy 3:16–17 KJV). God inspired the writers of both the Old and the New Testaments for the express purpose that the Bible could instruct, correct, and direct us onto the path of righteousness.

KNOWING GOD BY KNOWING HIS WORD

Respected theologian A. W. Tozer said: "God is not silent. It is the nature of God to speak. The second person in the Trinity is called 'The Word.' The Bible is the inevitable outcome of God's continuous speech. It is the infallible declaration of His mind."

God speaks and reveals Himself through His Word. He describes His character, qualities, desires, and plans. He gives us a glimpse into His background and "history." In short, He provides us with lots of information so we can know Him. We can approach the Bible not as a dry manuscript or history text, but as a way to develop closeness with our Father. God inspired His Book to be written and given to us that we may know Him intimately.

John Kass, a columnist for the *Chicago Tribune*, wrote about a waiter he met named Bouch, who worked at a tavern in Chicago. Bouch decided to write to the king of his homeland, Morocco. King Mohammed VI is immensely popular because he often interacts with his subjects in public, he has freed political prisoners, and he helps the poor and disabled. When Bouch wrote to him from the United States, King Mohammed VI, true to form, wrote back.

"Look at the letters," Bouch told Kass. "These are letters from the king. If I meet him, I'll be so happy."

In his column, Kass mused, "How many guys hauling beer and burgers in a Chicago tavern have a correspondence going with a royal monarch?"

The journalist was intrigued, so he talked to Morocco's deputy consul general in Chicago. Kass was told that it isn't unusual for the king to write personal letters to his subjects abroad.

"It happens a lot," the official told him. "The king loves his subjects."[1]

We fancy the idea that a king would correspond with a commoner. But there's something far more incredible. The King of kings, the Creator of the universe, has chosen to correspond with us. He has given us an entire book full of letters, stories, and poetry. The true King, the God of all creation, wants to communicate with you and me.

THE GREATEST LOVE STORY THE WORLD HAS EVER KNOWN

For many people throughout the centuries, the Bible has been known as a book about love. It is filled with passionate love stories in the Old Testament. It also tells about "lust stories." Our society is, of course, consumed with the subjects of sex and romance. These topics are found within the pages of the Bible from beginning to end. However, sex as God intended it is revealed in very healthy terms.

When you begin a fresh journey in the Scriptures, you will read of people from all walks of life, from all cultures, financial positions, and emotional states of mind. The Bible is blunt and honest, and it tells stories of rape and incest and adultery. Bible stories could actually fill many seasons of prime-time soap operas if the networks were interested.

However, the real love story contained in the Bible is found from the first page to the very last page of the book. It is almost as if it has to be deciphered much like a military code. But, thank God, you and I do not need to be cryptologists to unravel the mysteries of this fascinating book.

When you read the Bible, you learn very quickly that God loves His creation. It becomes obvious, and you can see He loved the people of the Bible from the first humans He created to the last generation of humans described in the Book of Revelation. Yes, Adam and Eve and their offspring have all been recipients of His wonderful love. It is mysterious, but it is something that, with a little bit of work on your part, you can understand and receive all the things God wants to tell you.

Make a commitment to yourself right now: "I want to know God, and I will be open to hearing from Him!" This book is written to make it easy for you to discover everything God has for you. He loves you so very much, and He is calling you to get to know Him in a deep and personal way. Listen to Saint John, one of the early apostles of Jesus Christ. He wrote the following words to the early believers:

> *The person who refuses to love doesn't know the*
> *first thing about God, because God is love—so you can't*
> *know him if you don't love (1 John 4:8 MSG).*

The fact that God is love opens the door for us to be loved by Him, and not only to love Him in return but also to love other people as well. That is a divine revelation that most people miss. Love is how we know whether God is in someone or not. I am sure that you know that there are a lot of very "religious" people who don't have an ounce of love within them. This fact of life may have been a stumbling block for you to believe in God. But let's work together to bring more of God's love into your life. It will take faith on your part.

Jesus said, "Search the scriptures; for in them ye think ye have eternal life: and they are they which testify of me" (John 5:39 KJV). Many people do search the Scriptures but never accept the Jesus of the Scriptures.

You and I want to be people who read the Scriptures, not to

dispute them, but rather to embrace them. The Bible is for today, it speaks of yesterday, but points the way for tomorrow. It is active and alive and thrilling to read. It is the means to draw you closer to God and His love for you.

Many years ago, a doting, devoted young husband named James Bracy got in the habit of writing love letters to his bride, Sallie. Stationed at a California military base during the 1950s, he was separated from her by thousands of miles. James' link to the lovely woman waiting for him to come home was their love letters, which they wrote with great care and consistency. But one of James' letters didn't get delivered. Somehow it was misplaced and became lodged between two walls in the mailroom at Fort Ord, an army base a few miles from Monterey, California. The letter was lost in the shadows, with its romantic affections of a youthful marriage, sealed with a kiss.

Jump ahead a half-century later. James and Sallie Bracy had just celebrated their fiftieth wedding anniversary and were relaxing in the living room when their song, "Once in a While," began to play on the radio. Sallie remembered affectionately the 1950s tune and how she used to get calls and letters from the man who owned her heart. They joked together, knowing there would be no letter or phone call this time because James was present in person, right by her side.

Meanwhile, a construction crew was dismantling the old post office at Fort Ord, and they discovered a long-forgotten letter from a young army corporal. The crew turned the letter over to Bob Spadoni, the postmaster in nearby Monterey. Spadoni began the process of delivering that letter, tracking down the Bracys through post office records and phone books.

Just a few days after hearing their song and enjoying their fiftieth anniversary, the letter dated January 28, 1955, was delivered to Sallie Bracy. The letter filled her heart with warmth and romance. Tears welled up in her eyes, and she again felt like that love-struck twenty-two-year-old from long ago.

"It meant a lot to me then," said Sallie. "It means even more now."[2]

Many years ago, God wrote His love letter to us. For some people, it's been forgotten or misplaced. But it's waiting to be delivered, to be opened at just the right time. When we read the words God wrote to us, our hearts will be filled with love and appreciation for Him. Everything about our lives will be changed for the better.

CHAPTER TWO

TAKE ANOTHER LOOK AT THE BOOK

WHY SO MANY PEOPLE HAVE A DISTORTED IMAGE OF THE BIBLE

Most people are bothered by those passages of Scripture they do not understand, but the passages that bother me are those I do understand.

MARK TWAIN

When I was young, I considered the Bible to be a book for old people. When I was an elementary and junior-high schoolboy, baseball and basketball were much more fun to me than reading a stuffy senior citizens' book. Of course, when it came to the teen years and high school, girls and popularity were the center of the known universe—at least my known universe.

What is it about the Bible that causes so many people to have a distorted image of it? Why is it often considered an "old people's" book? Why do boys and girls, men and women, frequently think it is boring, tedious, and dry?

An old story from Kentucky can shine some light on the uncomfortable feelings of the Bible, religion, and anything connected with it. A young priest went to the home of a family that had just joined his local parish. Everyone in the family was friendly toward him—except for the five-year-old daughter. Throughout dinner she continued to stare at the priest, sizing him up with obvious suspicion. Trying to make the little girl relax and accept him, he used a simple approach of honesty.

Turning to her, the priest asked, "Does my collar make you uncomfortable? Is that what you are staring at?"

He removed his clerical collar from around his neck and held it out for her to see. When it came off, he happened to notice the cleaning instructions on the inside of the collar, and to continue his conversation, he asked the girl, "Do you know what this says right here on my collar?"

"Yes, I do," the girl replied matter-of-factly. "It says, 'Kills fleas for six months.'"

Of course, children and grown-ups alike often regard matters of religion and faith with a degree of suspicion. They may mistrust "institutionalized religion." They may doubt the motives of leaders. They may avoid believers who are pushy and judgmental. They may question the relevance and authority of the Bible. Why is this? Where do these suspicions originate? Let's look at a few common causes.

BAD CHILDHOOD EXPERIENCES

Most of us arrive at adulthood with a mix of painful childhood memories and wonderful recollections. More and more, our society is falling apart, and children are the ones paying the price. They not only pay for problems and sufferings at the time, but also for years after when they are left with scars and deep wounds from painful experiences.

I cannot imagine any deception inflicted upon a child more insidious than to have a church leader or member misuse or abuse a child. That has to be one of the worst acts perpetrated upon mankind. Tragically, news reports like this one have become almost commonplace:

> FOR MANY PEOPLE, CHILDHOOD HURTS HAVE HINDERED THEIR SPIRITUAL GROWTH AS ADULTS.

U.S. Catholic bishops on Tuesday claimed progress against sexual abuse, but word of 800 new molestation lawsuits in California courts indicated the church has yet to put the two-year scandal behind it. The crisis spread to every American diocese. Since then, more than 1,000 people have come forward with abuse allegations against dioceses across the country. The charges have led to large financial claims against the church, the resignation of top officials and the prosecution of priests.[1]

I believe the vast majority of church leaders care deeply about their members, and they sincerely try to promote the spiritual, emotional, and physical health of those they serve. But abuse and mistreatment does happen—that is the tragic reality of the world we live in. And when it does happen, lives are left shattered.

Recently my friend Lauren told our church her story of finding salvation. She is a beautiful young woman who went to church all of her life. Her grandmother and grandfather are devout and loving Christian people. Her parents took her to Sunday school and to the church youth group regularly, and she attended a good Christian school growing up. She was not a stranger to the Bible or the promises it contains.

After Lauren told about her consistent church attendance and religious upbringing, this poised, twenty-something woman shocked the audience. She told how a date rape had set her on a course of anger, disappointment, and disillusionment. She could not understand how that could have happened to her. She had always tried to do the right things and be a good person.

To cover up her pain and bitterness, Lauren began drinking, taking drugs, and having sex with boyfriends over the next several years. But, not surprisingly, she only felt worse and worse about herself. The torment seemed as if it would never end for this precious woman. I do not know if you have wrestled with something this painful before, but can't you sense the great anguish in the heart of this dear person?

Lauren did her best for years to play the role of the beautiful, bright, Christian college student. Earning good grades was easy for someone so intelligent. Athletics came naturally, too. And she had many friends, since she was always considered the life of the party. Deep down, however, there was misery and suffering for the girl whose sorority sisters envied her striking beauty and bubbly personality.

Then it happened. God intervened at a time when she was

searching for her roots. A weekly Bible study in the home of a friend drew her and dozens of college-age kids together. The music, teaching, and fellowship were all rich with the love of God. It was "her time" and "her place." The Holy Spirit penetrated her heart. He broke through to the deepest hurt in her life, just like He can do for you.

Lauren's life began to turn around, and she experienced deep-down happiness for the first time in many years. I'm not suggesting this was all a quick fix for her. She still had much healing to do with the help of a counselor and trusted friends. Most of all, it was the consistent study of the Scriptures that gave Lauren a clear understanding of herself and her purpose for living. You see, Jesus told His disciples that God would use the Holy Spirit to lead all of His children in their daily lives. As Jesus promised, "When he, the Spirit of truth, comes, he will guide you into all truth. He will not speak on his own; he will speak only what he hears, and he will tell you what is yet to come" (John 16:13).

Perhaps you have not had a terrible experience like Lauren did. Something of that magnitude may not have kept you from the Bible. But even experiences far less traumatic might have hurt you as a child to the point that you would never want to read the Bible, let alone have anything to do with God. For many people, childhood hurts have hindered their spiritual growth as adults. For others, the church has in some way wounded or misled them, so they are not comfortable with anything related to religion, including the Bible.

Yet God is the God of love, and He patiently waits for the opportunity to lead and guide us to the truth. He waits for "our time" and "our place" until we will call out to Him and are saved.

CULTURAL AND SOCIETAL IMPRESSIONS

Other people have a distorted view of the Bible because of something that is, in some cases, harder to get past than a childhood hurt. I'm referring to cultural and societal influences that form our impressions and beliefs. That doesn't necessarily mean the ethnic and national customs of a particular country give people a distorted image of the Bible. I mean that the values, morals, ethics, and mores within any culture can dramatically shape one's thinking.

THE BIBLE ISN'T A BOOK THAT SAYS, "NO, YOU CAN'T!" IT'S A BOOK THAT SAYS, "YES, YOU CAN!"

Our media-saturated American culture, for instance, tells us that the primary pursuits in life should be wealth, fame, and power. That's quite different from what Jesus told His followers: "Blessed are the poor in spirit. Blessed are the meek. Blessed are the merciful" (see Matthew 5). Our society says you can pick any ol' god to follow—after all, they're pretty much the same. The important thing is to choose some deity to make your own. But Jesus told His listeners: "I am the way, the truth, and the life. No one comes to the Father except through Me" (John 14:6 NKJV). You can see how the prevailing messages of our society are contrary to the messages of the Bible.

Sometimes culture happens on a smaller scale. Many college students tell me how their professors rail against religion, especially Christianity and the Bible. Standing up for their faith would subject these students to withering ridicule and mockery. Obviously, the culture of these campuses opposes and discredits the Bible.

Other times the religious culture that people have grown up in greatly influences their view of the Bible. Muslim nations have a view that doesn't clearly represent the Bible, simply because their faith is in the book they believe in, the Quran. A Hindu may have heard of the Bible but was probably taught it is a religious book written for and by Jews and Christians. They could not grasp the relevancy of it for their lives.

Similarly, many Korean people, either in the North or the South, have been influenced by shamanism and therefore have developed an inaccurate image of the Holy Spirit. This might be because the spirit of shamanism blends in with their personal beliefs about the Holy Spirit described in the Bible.

In an article titled "Shamanistic Influences in Korean Pentecostal Christianity," Jeremy Reynalds points out:

> *Korean Christians tend to see Christianity as a path to material prosperity. That trait is a residue of shamanism, the native folk religion for centuries in Korea and other Northeast Asian countries. In shamanism, the shaman (a quasi-medicine man or woman) is asked to intercede with the spirits to ensure one's health or business success. Many professing Christians contend that the gods of shamanism and the God of Christianity are kindred spirits.*[2]

On the other hand, we know that the God of the Bible transcends cultural distortions and mythology. Korea has a large and robust Christian community—people who wholeheartedly affirm the Bible's authority and accuracy. They passionately live out their faith in God and dedication to Jesus.

What I find fascinating is the concept of cross-cultural mission. You might think that God would use only local Christian people to present the Gospel and accurate translations of the Bible to speak to each nation. But God sends His messengers to every country and tribe—no matter how isolated—to make sure they hear about His love for them. Millions of His people crisscross the globe, breaching cultural and language barriers every day of the week. This occurs on a daily basis without any central clearinghouse or principal mission agency.

I can tell you why I believe this goes on twenty-four hours a day, seven days a week: It is because of the love depicted in the Holy Scriptures and love for the God described in its pages. Yes, we would agree that cultural and societal issues can distort our impressions of the Bible, but the God of the Bible is bigger than any society, bigger than any culture, and definitely bigger than any distortion. Supernaturally, He is able to communicate to every person who inhabits our "third rock from the sun."

According to the International Programs Center, a division of the U.S. Census Bureau, the total population of the world as of this writing is 6,345,266,678. By the time you read this, the figure will have increased by several million.[3] When we view the present-day world population, it is obvious that God has a monumental job on His hands. How can He communicate to so many people scattered around so many countries? The Bible is His vehicle of truth and instruction for every nation. So He calls upon people from all cultures to help His project move forward.

Despite the unfathomable number of people who inhabit the earth, God's love is still speaking to multilingual, multi-cultured peoples everywhere.

A BOOK OF DOS AND DON'TS

When I was in junior high, some kids in my class attended the Baptist church across the street from our school. They invited me to join their youth group and play on their church basketball team. I thought that would be neat, since several of the cool kids in our class went to that church.

Though I didn't have a church background or an understanding of religion, I did have a bias against the Bible. My primary prejudice was the same that many people have. See if you can identify with the prevailing prejudice of my youth: "The Bible is nothing but a book of dos and don'ts." Does that sound familiar to you?

Of course, I formed that negative viewpoint without actually reading the Bible. Thankfully, I have learned from personal experience that the "dos and don'ts" claim could not be further from the truth. The Bible is, in fact, a book that teaches us how to live a blessed life. It isn't a book that says, "No, you can't!" It's a book that says, "Yes, you can!" It details for its readers the keys to successful spiritual living. It tells how to develop happy relationships, how to find fulfillment, and how to live a meaningful life.

Over the years, the misconception about dos and don'ts has become clearer to me. Many misinformed people (including me as a young person) equate the Bible with the Ten Commandments. And they think those Old Testament commandments exist just to prevent them from doing things that appear fun. People who want an excuse to avoid the Bible usually refer to this limited section of Scripture, which they probably have heard about but not actually read.

In reality, those "thou shalt not" statements of the *King James Bible* are not negative in the normal meaning of the term. They contain the words of a loving Father, who is warning His children to keep away from things that may hurt or ultimately destroy them.

When Sandy and I were looking for a new home in the 1970s, we searched for six months in just about every San Diego-area community to find the best place to raise our children and begin our ministry. We settled on three priorities: price first, house second, location third. The right price meant that we could squeak by with the monthly expense. The right house meant it could accommodate our large, rambunctious family. The right location meant our boundary would be the outskirts of San Diego—no more than a forty-minute drive to and from home to work. Eventually, we found a place that met all three conditions.

But the right location also brought a drawback: rattlesnakes. Hot and dry describes the community we lived in. The neighborhood had been carved out of hills, gullies, and old riverbeds. It was situated in the natural habitat of these poisonous reptiles. Since venomous snakes are not on the top of my "to invite" list, I said to the Lord, "If ever a rattlesnake comes onto our property, I am moving."

One day while we were checking on the construction of the house, I walked to the edge of our property line in the backyard. Beyond stretched miles and miles of undeveloped land, with nothing but natural scrub brush, dirt, rocks, and hills. The area was filled with coyotes, ground squirrels, mice, and, you guessed it, rattlesnakes.

Walking up to the barrier the county had securely planted at the property line, I noticed a four- or five-foot rattlesnake dangling from top to bottom on that barricade. A closer look showed that the head and rattles were missing. Later, one of the carpenters told me he had killed the snake and taken the bounty home.

Okay, that was close, but it wasn't on our property. The construction of the house continued, and we moved in. Our family ended up staying in that little "starter" home for ten years.

When it came time to move closer to our new church location, we sold that house. The week we were to close escrow and move, Sandy called me at the church office to say a rattlesnake had come onto our property and the fire department was trying to capture it. Now that was definitely on our property, and I did not mind leaving.

> CHILDREN AND
> GROWN-UPS ALIKE
> OFTEN REGARD
> MATTERS OF
> RELIGION AND
> FAITH WITH A
> DEGREE OF
> SUSPICION.

I tell you this story because during the ten years we lived there, our five children were young. At one point, all five of them were under the age of ten. Sandy and I wanted this curious, adventurous, investigative brood to know that rattlesnakes are dangerous! We often warned, "Do not pick up snakes. ... Let Mom or Dad know if you come across one. ... Stay away from anything that slithers." Our bottom-line message: "Do not play with rattlesnakes!" Does that sound unreasonable to you?

This story makes the point concerning the dos and the don'ts of the Bible. As loving parents, Sandy and I did not want something that may have looked intriguing or fun to harm our much-loved children. We wanted them to be safe, healthy, and happy. This had to be the same heartfelt intent of the Creator when He issued the "thou shalt not" statements. It was for our own good.

God gave Moses the Ten Commandments. When Moses came down the mountain with these commandments etched in stone, he knew God had given each command in love, not in anger. The Ten Commandments have been important to every Christian civilization that has existed from that time forward. Why? Because the foundation of strong societies has been preserved by the content of those two stone tablets in the arms of Moses.

Six commandments deal with people getting along with others; the other four commandments deal with people getting along with God. It seems to be a simple matter of mathematics, doesn't it? It takes more work to get along with people than it does to get along with God. Those commandments were not written by a fist-shaking God, but rather by a loving Father who didn't want His children to get bitten by the snake.

Let me help you to say good-bye to the dos-and-don'ts myth, which has been perpetrated by the Devil himself. Read carefully the description of the Devil:

> *There was war in heaven. Michael and his angels fought against the dragon, and the dragon and his angels fought back. But he was not strong enough, and they lost their place in heaven. The great dragon was hurled down—that ancient serpent called the devil, or*

Satan, who leads the whole world astray (Revelation 12:7–9).

That's right—the Devil is called the "ancient serpent." He is trying to keep people from the Bible because it holds the answers to life while he holds the answers for death. Next, we come to the most important part:

> *Then I heard a loud voice saying in heaven, "Now salvation, and strength, and the kingdom of our God, and the power of His Christ have come, for the accuser of our brethren, who accused them before our God day and night, has been cast down. And they overcame him by the blood of the Lamb and by the word of their testimony and they did not love their lives to the death"* (Revelation 12:10–11 NKJV).

These verses tell you some positive things, one of which is that salvation can be yours. You can live for eternity with God. Second, it tells you that strength can be yours. You can make it through life and all of its obstacles. These great Bible verses say that Jesus shed His blood for you, so you could live forever with God. In other words, He died in your place. When you believe in Jesus and declare your faith in Him, the work of the Devil is overcome.

Your acceptance of Jesus is all God requires. When a person repents of all sin and receives Jesus as Lord, he or she has access to the Father. It is only faith that can ultimately save your soul. But it is vital that you have your faith directed toward the right place. Listen to the words of the apostle Paul:

If you confess with your mouth, "Jesus is Lord,"
and believe in your heart that God raised him from the
dead, you will be saved. For it is with your heart that
you believe and are justified, and it is with your mouth
that you confess and are saved. As the Scripture says,
"Anyone who trusts in him will never be put to shame"
(Romans 10:9–11).

The Devil would have you believe that the Bible is full of rules and regulations to spoil all your fun. God tells us just the opposite: The Bible is full of stories and principles that will bring us fulfillment, contentment, and satisfaction.

OUTDATED AND IRRELEVANT

Here's something I've heard countless times over the years: "Sure, the Bible is great literature—imaginative stories, inspirational ideas, nice poetry. But it's archaic and outdated. It's an old book for olden times, not relevant for today." As a matter of fact, I used to say that, though I had never turned a page of the Bible.

You may find this concept liberating: Jesus never once mentioned that the Scriptures handed down to the people of His time were outdated or irrelevant. That is interesting, because He quoted verses over and over in His sermons, teachings, and discourses.

Jesus actually quoted from several sources of what we call the Old Testament, including the books of Moses, the Psalms, and the Prophets. In the New Testament, we read how the Jewish leaders, called Pharisees, tried to trick Him with a question about divorce. His response was, "Haven't you read ... that at the beginning the Creator 'made them male and female,' and said, 'For this reason a man will leave his father and mother and be united to his wife, and the two will become one flesh'?" (Matthew 19:4–5).

Later, speaking about when the history of mankind will end, He referred to Noah, the Flood, and God's judgment (see Matthew 24:37–39). And in the following text, we see Jesus' familiarity with many Old Testament characters:

> *A wicked and adulterous generation asks for a miraculous sign! But none will be given it except the sign of the prophet Jonah. For as Jonah was three days and three nights in the belly of a huge fish, so the Son of Man will be three days and three nights in the heart of the earth. … The Queen of the South will rise at the judgment with this generation and condemn it; for she came from the ends of the earth to listen to Solomon's wisdom, and now one greater than Solomon is here* (Matthew 12:39–40, 42).

Jesus mentioned Isaiah, Elijah, Daniel, Abel, Zechariah, Abiathar, Isaac, and Jacob in the messages He preached. Jesus didn't merely allude to these people and their stories; He made the events and persons factual to history. Indeed, most of the items Jesus quoted or cited were controversial subjects, such as Creation or Noah's Flood, not to mention Jonah and the great fish.

THE BIBLE IS FULL OF STORIES AND PRINCIPLES THAT WILL BRING US FULFILLMENT, CONTENTMENT, AND SATISFACTION.

If the Scriptures were relevant to Jesus approximately four thousand years after the time of Adam, Abraham, Noah, and the others, don't you think the Bible could be relevant to you today? I realize that some may argue that Jesus is a historical figure who lived two thousand years ago, so why would that make the Bible relevant to me today? I would like to encourage you that when a person gets to know Jesus, he or she will know that His words are true—and timeless. The writer of the book of Hebrews said: "Jesus Christ is the same yesterday, and today, and for ever" (13:8 KJV). This tells us that what was relevant for humankind from the beginning of time until Jesus' time and is still relevant today. You see, a man still faces the same basic problems today in Manhattan as men faced in ancient Babylon; the issues that a woman in Paris faces today are the same problems women in Egypt would have faced. Those same problems and issues of the human heart that have always been a problem are the same issues you face today as you read this book.

The blessing of Scripture is that it is for all times, all people, in all cultures.

TREASURE FOR THE TAKING

When I was younger, it always seemed like an overwhelming project to try to get to God. So why try? There were fun things to do, cool people to meet, lots of money to be made. An untold number of romantic and challenging distant ports were waiting to be discovered. I told myself, I'll worry about reading the Bible and settling things with God when I am old and lonely and dying. That seems like the philosophy of many people throughout the centuries, in countless countries around the world.

With all the blessings and benefits afforded us by the Bible, it is sad that so many people in our politically correct world try to discount and disregard the truth of God's Word. Others attempt to keep the Bible out of the hands of people. Try to teach the Bible in a public school setting. You're asking for trouble. Try to post the Ten Commandments or other Scriptures in a courthouse. Expect a backlash. Many so-called experts feel the Bible is a problem and should not be endorsed by governmental or educational institutions. As a result, a large percentage of people never read God's Word, since they view it as irrelevant, outmoded, or obsolete.

Many other people turn to the Bible only in times of extreme crisis or when death appears to be approaching. W. C. Fields, one of America's most famous comedians from the last century, was known not only for his quick wit but also for his lifelong alcohol problem. In fact, much of Mr. Fields' humor appeared to center on alcohol use and abuse. On his deathbed, Fields was visited by a friend who was surprised to find him reading the Bible. His old friend looked at him and asked, "Why, you old atheist. What are you doing reading that? You're not worried, are you?"

"No, no," Fields replied. "Just looking for loopholes."

Personally, I feel sorry for those who claim the Bible is false and for those who use it only to find "loopholes." Those who read it only in emergency situations are shortchanging themselves. They are being deprived of the blessings the Bible brings to a civilized or uncivilized world. They are missing opportunities to hear from the Creator of the universe, the loving Father.

If you are someone who reads the Bible regularly, then

carry on. Enjoy all the good things God is revealing to you. If you are someone who resists the Bible, ask yourself why this is. Where does your resistance come from? Take an honest, clear-eyed look at your background and within your heart. For I believe that anyone who avoids the Bible is missing the greatest treasure found on planet earth.

THE PARADIGM OF PRIVILEGE

BIBLE READING IS NOT A "HAVE TO" BUT A "GET TO"

Draw the honey out of the comb of Scripture, and live on its sweetness.
CHARLES H. SPURGEON

Let's suppose you were conducting a survey to determine what people really thought about the Bible. And let's say you went downtown with clipboard in hand and asked passersby, "What one adjective would you use to describe the Bible?"

I'm guessing the common responses you would receive might include *boring, outdated, dull, old-fashioned, fuddy-duddy, uptight.* Perhaps a few folks would use adjectives such as *intriguing, interesting, inspirational,* or *transcendent.*

Now let's say you wanted to segment your survey to zero

in on churchgoers. So you drive around and stop at the first church you come across. You stand outside the sanctuary and ask the same question you posed before. If you assured these people they would remain anonymous, and if they knew their responses were strictly confidential, I bet you'd hear some of the similar answers that the downtown folks gave (boring, dull, old-fashioned) but with a few more positive descriptors thrown in: helpful, encouraging, uplifting, comforting, instructive.

Here's my point: If you received a hundred responses from people giving one-word descriptions of the Bible, you might get a couple that included words such as:

Fun

Riveting

Fascinating

Thrilling

Exhilarating

Stunning

Astonishing

Spellbinding

It's too bad that more people don't think of the Bible in these superlative terms, because it can be the most powerful, potent, spine-tingling book you will ever read. If you relish the suspense of a well-written thriller, if you appreciate the guidance offered by a thought-provoking self-help book, if you enjoy the intrigue of a first-rate whodunit, if you savor the imagery and emotion found in fine poetry, then you should absolutely love the Bible. It is all of those things and more rolled into one life-changing, awe-inspiring volume.

Let's take a look at the Bible in possibly a new light for you. Let's set aside our old presumptions and come at the Bible with a fresh approach. Be assured that I am not someone who has a flippant or casual perspective of the Bible; in fact, I have the utmost respect and reverence for it. Yet in all of my years of studying the Bible on my own, researching it in graduate school, and teaching it for several decades, I can honestly say I have fun reading the Scriptures. When was the last time you heard someone call Bible reading fun? Beyond

> **WHEN WE COME TO SEE THE VALUE OF THE HOLY SCRIPTURES, WE WILL KNOW THAT GOD'S BOOK IS NOT A BURDEN BUT A BLESSING.**

the enjoyment I gain from reading the Scriptures, I find them deeply meaningful and significant. No single activity has been more life-changing for me than hearing the Creator of the universe speak to me through His Word.

I have found that reading the Bible is not an obligatory "have to" but an awesome "get to." Often the message of Scripture leaps off the pages of the black leather book as if propelled by a slingshot. Other times I need a pick and a shovel to break through the meaning of Scripture. But, boy, oh boy, when the meaning becomes clear to me, it's like finding the mother lode in a mountain full of gold. Nothing says it any clearer than one of the psalms of David:

> *The law of the LORD is perfect, converting the soul;*
> *The testimony of the LORD is sure, making wise the simple;*

The statutes of the LORD are right, rejoicing the heart;
The commandment of the Lord is pure, enlightening
  the eyes;
The fear of the LORD is clean, enduring forever;
The judgments of the LORD are true and righteous
  altogether.
More to be desired are they than gold,
Yea, than much fine gold;
Sweeter also than honey and the honeycomb
(Psalm 19:7–10 NKJV).

If we don't consider the Bible more desired than gold and sweeter than honey, maybe we're missing something. Maybe, just maybe, it's our *attitude* toward the Bible and not the Bible itself that is dreary and negative. Maybe it's time for a new way of looking at things.

MAKE A SHIFT, GET A LIFT

Years ago while attending graduate school, I found myself writing lots of papers and reading dozens of books. During that time, I was introduced to a word that had not previously been part of my vocabulary—*paradigm*. I like to think of its pronunciation as a "pair of dimes." I also discovered this word is often used in connection with the word *shift*.

WHATEVER YOUR PARTICULAR INTEREST IN READING— POETRY, HISTORY, LOVE STORIES— THE BIBLE OFFERS PLENTY TO SATISFY YOU.

Chances are you've heard the term *paradigm shift* because it is frequently used—perhaps overused—in our modern vernacular. But back when I stumbled across the term, it was a relative newcomer to the English lexicon. Futurists and visionaries such as Alvin Toffler in his work *The Third Wave* and John Nesbitt in *Megatrends* were both proponents of a paradigm shift. They were like prophets telling the world where we would be in the twenty-first century.

Later, Stephen Covey, in his best-selling book *Seven Habits of Highly Effective People*, applied the paradigm-shift principle to business and to people's personal lives. If you were to go online and "Ask Jeeves" what *paradigm* means, you will find it is a "shared set of assumptions and perspectives; a framework, held in common, used to interpret reality; a set of rules and regulations that establish boundaries, and that tell us what to do to be successful within those boundaries."

A paradigm shift, then, is a radical change in perspective. You take a belief, philosophy, or assumption and turn it upside down. Covey says that paradigms are like roadmaps that lead us in a certain direction:

> *Each of us has many, many maps in our head [and] we interpret everything we experience through these mental maps. We seldom question their accuracy; we're usually even unaware that we have them. We simply assume that the way we see things is the way they really are or the way they should be. And our attitudes and behaviors grow out of these assumptions. The way we see things is the source of the way we think and the way we act.*[1]

He goes on to say:

Paradigms are powerful because they create the lens through which we see the world. The power of a paradigm shift is the essential power of quantum change, whether that shift is instantaneous or a slow and deliberate process.[2]

Why am I providing all this background on paradigms? Because many people need to shift their "set of assumptions and perspectives," which often are negative concerning the Bible. What if we could truly view the Bible as a blessing rather than a burden, a treasure rather than a task? Would it change the way we approach God's book—and even God Himself? I'm convinced it would.

During the 1970s and 1980s, long before the Berlin Wall fell or communism was uprooted in Russia and other Iron Curtain countries, I traveled through Eastern Europe teaching in "underground" Bible studies. The communist governments were strictly—and often violently—opposed to Bibles and Bible studies. They believed the manifesto "Religion is the opiate of the people" and a threat to government rule. It was during those times in Hungary, Czechoslovakia, Romania, Poland, East Germany, and Russia that I began to understand the difficulties of Christian people and Bible believers. Today, that paradigm has shifted, since communism has largely crumbled throughout the world, with only a few iron-fisted holdouts left.

For the Bible believers living in repressed areas of the world, the Bible was an incredible privilege to own or possess. When they heard the Bible read, they sat in rapt attention.

When they heard the Bible taught, they hung on every word. This heartfelt, appreciative attitude is needed once again in modern-day society.

Dr. Bill Bright, the founder of Campus Crusade for Christ, told a story of a famous Texas oil field called Yates Pool. During the Depression, this field was a sheep ranch named after its owner, Mr. Yates. Unfortunately, he wasn't able to make enough on his ranching operation to pay the principal and interest on the mortgage, so he was in danger of losing his ranch. With little money for clothes and food, his family, like many others during that time, relied on government subsidy to survive.

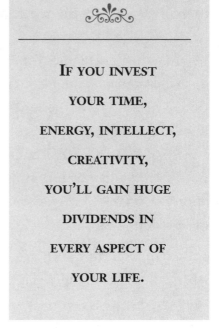

IF YOU INVEST YOUR TIME, ENERGY, INTELLECT, CREATIVITY, YOU'LL GAIN HUGE DIVIDENDS IN EVERY ASPECT OF YOUR LIFE.

Day after day, as Yates grazed his sheep over those rolling West Texas hills, he must have been greatly troubled about how to pay his bills. Then one day, a seismographic crew from an oil company came into the area and told him there might be oil on his land. They asked permission to drill a wildcat well, and he signed a lease contract.

At 1,115 feet, the crew struck a huge oil reserve. The first well came in at 80,000 barrels a day. Many subsequent wells were more than twice as large. In fact, thirty years after the discovery, a government test of one of the wells showed it still had the potential flow of 125,000 barrels of oil a day.

And Mr. Yates owned it all. The day he purchased the land

he had received the oil and mineral rights. Yet he'd been living on government support. Imagine, a multimillionaire living in poverty. What was the problem? He didn't know the oil was there even though he owned it.[3]

Do you think that Mr. Yates underwent a paradigm shift in regard to his ranchland? You bet he did! One day he saw it as dry and unproductive; the next day, he couldn't believe his good fortune. This is exactly the kind of turnaround many people need toward the Bible. They view it as dry and unproductive, not realizing that it is a source of untold wealth and riches. If you are in need of a paradigm shift in regard to the Bible—if you want to approach it each day with enthusiasm rather than disatisfaction or boredom—consider the following ideas.

Invest Yourself in the Bible—and Reap Rewards

Abraham Lincoln once said, "People are about as happy as they choose to be." In other words, those who want to be fulfilled and content with their lives usually find a way to make it happen. They develop an optimistic outlook, identify goals and steadily work toward them, and seek ways to grow and improve. It's a matter of attitude and determination.

The same principle holds true in our approach to the Bible. If we expect it to be dull and dry, guess what? We'll probably experience it as dull and dry, just like that land above the rich oil that was sitting below. But what if we come to the Bible with high expectations, anticipating that it will grip our minds, stir our hearts, and capture our imaginations? If we believe those things are going happen, they surely will.

Let's paraphrase Lincoln's quote for our discussion: "People get out of the Bible about as much as they choose to." Reading the Bible is only as tedious and boring as you make it; it can and should be the most exciting, captivating book you own. If you invest yourself in it—your time, energy, intellect, creativity— you'll gain huge dividends in every aspect of your life.

Feed Your Fascination

The Bible offers something for everyone, and it supplies plenty of substance for each person's particular interests and inclinations. For instance, some people are drawn to interesting, imaginative stories—tales of drama, daring-do, and skullduggery. The Scriptures contain stories more spellbinding than anything written by Shakespeare, Homer, Tolstoy, or Melville— let alone modern writers such as Stephen King or John Grisham. What makes the biblical stories all the more enthralling is that they're absolutely true.

Other people are drawn to vivid characters and powerful personalities—flesh-and-blood people who prevailed against impossible odds, enjoyed great romance, or simply did the right thing when their backs were against the wall. The Bible is full of the most despicable villains, the most triumphant heroes, and everything in between. If you want to boost your enjoyment of the Scriptures, identify a favorite character and do an in-depth study of that person.

As for me, I often find myself intrigued by the structure and makeup of the Bible—particularly the "coincidences of composition," which are surely not coincidences at all. Consider that the shortest chapter in the Bible is Psalm 117, and the longest chapter is Psalm 119. Psalm 118 is the center chapter of the entire Bible. So we have the middle chapter of the Bible wedged between the shortest and longest chapters. This "mild phenomenon" gets more compelling when you realize that there are 594 chapters through Psalm 118 and exactly 594 chapters after Psalm 118. When you add up all the chapters of the Bible, you end up with 1188. Did you know that the center verse of the Bible is Psalm 118:8?

To me this is all very fascinating. It makes my mind become inquisitive and investigative. One cannot but think that the God of the Bible was behind this creative literary construction. For years books have been written on "Bible codes." Surely you can see that Psalm 118:8 is some kind of code. What mysterious message is contained in the center verse of the center chapter of the Bible? Let's take a closer look at this mysterious message in Psalm 118:8:

THE BIBLE CAN BE THE MOST POWERFUL, POTENT, SPINE-TINGLING BOOK YOU WILL EVER READ.

"It is better to trust in the LORD than to put confidence in man."

That, my friends, is the cryptic code of this fabulous find of Scripture. If you were to decipher this code, you would realize the message is simply this: Trust God. We can definitely see that our confidence in man is shaken after centuries of watching the destruction of humankind. So, instead of putting our confidence in man and his institutions, the paradigm shift would be to put our trust in God.

Whatever your particular interest in reading—poetry, history, love stories—the Bible offers plenty to satisfy you. In the process, you'll learn more about this God who asks us to trust Him with our lives.

Cultivate an Attitude of Thankfulness

Saint Paul recognized the power of developing gratitude, joy, and thankfulness. His writings are peppered with phrases such as "Be joyful" and "In all things, give thanks." He wrote a letter to a community of believers in Colosse, saying, "Let the word of Christ dwell in you richly as you teach and admonish one another with all wisdom, and as you sing psalms, hymns and spiritual songs with gratitude in your hearts to God" (3:16). Perhaps Paul understood the human tendency to take gifts for granted or to have appreciation wane as time goes by. Surely, he also understood that a paradigm of thankfulness and appreciation enables us to fully enjoy God and His Word. An attitude of entitlement and ingratitude, meanwhile, might very well cause us to disregard the gift of the Bible.

The famous newspaper columnist Abigail van Buren, better known as "Dear Abby," told a story about a young man from a wealthy family who was about to graduate from high school. It was the custom in their affluent community for parents to give their graduating children a new car. This boy and his dad spent weeks visiting one dealership after another. The week before graduation, they found the perfect car. The boy was certain it would be in the driveway on graduation night.

On the eve of his graduation, however, his father handed him a small package wrapped in colorful paper. The father said the package contained the most valuable gift he could think of. It was a Bible. The boy was so disappointed and angry, he threw the Bible down and stormed out of the house. As events unfolded, he and his father never saw each other again.

Several years later, the news of the father's death finally brought the son home again. Following the funeral, he sat alone one evening going through his father's possessions that he was to inherit. He came across the Bible his dad had given him. Overwhelmed by grief, he brushed away the dust and cracked it open for the first time. When he did, a cashier's check dated the day of his high school graduation fell into his lap—in the exact amount of the car they had chosen together. The gift had been there all along … but he had turned away.[4]

Some people today totally reject God's gift of the Bible; far more receive it with reluctance. When we come to see the value of the Holy Scriptures—how it enriches our lives in every way—we will know that His book is not a burden but a blessing.

Surround Yourself with Those Who Love the Bible

The Old Testament book of Nehemiah features one of the classic biblical stories about falling in love with the Bible. To put it in context, the Jews had been taken captive by Nebuchadnezzar, the notorious leader of the Babylonian Empire. Babylon is located in present-day Iraq (before Saddam Hussein was ousted from power, he claimed to be Nebuchadnezzar and the ruler of Iraq and Babylon). For seventy years, the Jews lived in Babylon and adapted to the worldly culture. They underwent a collective "reprogramming" of beliefs and religion—a negative kind of paradigm shift. When the Jews were finally released at the end of their seventy-year captivity, only fifty thousand returned to Jerusalem to re-establish their homeland and culture. Nehemiah and Ezra were burdened to rebuild the walls of the city, restore the city gates, and reeducate the people about the Law of God. The following verses tell us about one of the first public readings of the Scriptures:

Now all the people gathered together as one man in the open square that was in front of the Water Gate; and they told Ezra the scribe to bring the Book of the Law of Moses, which the LORD had commanded Israel. So Ezra the priest brought the Law before the assembly of men and women and all who could hear with understanding on the first day of the seventh month. Then he read from it in the open square that was in front of the Water Gate from morning until midday, before the men and women and those who could understand; and the ears of all the people were attentive to the Book of the Law. So Ezra the scribe stood on a platform of wood which they had made for the purpose; and beside him, at his right hand, stood [many men]. ... And Ezra opened the book in the sight of all the people, for he was standing above all the people; and when he opened it, all the people stood up. And Ezra blessed the LORD, the great God. Then all the people answered, "Amen, Amen!" while lifting up their hands. And they bowed their heads and worshiped the LORD with their faces to the ground. [The leaders] helped the people to understand the Law; and the people stood in their place. So they read distinctly from the book, in the Law of God; and they gave the sense, and helped them to understand the reading (Nehemiah 8:1–8 NKJV).

Here are just a few highlights from this text: The Law of Moses was in written form and given to Ezra; Ezra openly read the Scriptures in the public square; everyone who was old enough to understand (men, women, and children) listened to the reading. The people were attentive to the reading for several hours—from morning until noon; they stood when the book was opened, and they bowed their heads as it was read, demonstrating reverence and respect for God and His Book. Certain men were gifted to instruct the people and understand what they had just heard from the Bible.

Drawing upon these insights, my suggestion is to regularly spend time with people who love and revere the Bible. Enthusiasm is contagious, and when you associate with folks who are excited about Scripture, your own level of excitement is sure to grow. Involve yourself with friends and neighbors in a home fellowship. Find coworkers or fellow students who will meet during the lunch hour or break time and read the Scriptures together. God will honor your desire to learn, and He will speak to you through the Bible.

Next, find a trusted, respected teacher to help you better understand and apply the Scriptures. Saint Paul told the early Christian community in Ephesus that God has endowed some people with a unique gift to understand and teach the Bible: "[God] gave some to be apostles, some prophets, some evangelists, and some pastors and teachers, for the equipping of the saints for the work of ministry, for the edifying of the body of Christ" (Ephesians 4:11–12 NKJV).

The purpose of their gift of understanding is not to make them superstars, but rather superservants. Their whole purpose in life is to help you and me understand how to live and grow as a child of God. In light of this, if you are not in a healthy, loving church that teaches the Bible, pray and ask God to lead you to one of His called teachers, a teacher who will help you understand the Scriptures.

First and Foremost, Look to the Book

In the course of writing this book, I have been tending to the needs of my ninety-one-year-old mother, who has encountered health problems. She has been hospitalized and given skilled nursing care to rehabilitate her. During this process, Sandy and I, along with my brother, have been trying to make Mom's transition from home to hospital as comfortable as possible.

While cleaning out closets and drawers in my mother's home, we came across her photograph collection of our family history. This was such a blessing to me, because I have little recollection of childhood. Nor do my brother or I have many pictures of our growing-up years. Along with the photos, we discovered my eighth-grade yearbook. Talk about a trip down memory lane! There before me were all the friends and classmates I spent time with as a kid. It was fun to remember them and the influence they had on me when I was growing up.

Leafing through the old yearbook, I spotted one classmate who was a close buddy in sixth through tenth grades. His name is Dewey Goff. During the time of our friendship, both his mother and my brother passed away. The common experience of death bound our youthful lives together. We rebelliously smoked our first Marlboros together and told each other our deep secrets and fears. With our jeans hanging low on our twelve-year-old hips and the sleeves of our white T-shirts rolled up our skinny beanpole arms, we would laugh together and struggle over our losses. What a gift to have that kind of mutual understanding and sympathy.

I recall a particular incident with Dewey. One hot summer evening, we sat together on the curb in front of my apartment building. We were discussing life and death and the meaning of it all. This was heavy stuff for a couple of kids, and we were obviously grappling with the hardship that had befallen us. Suddenly, Dewey said: "Let's go to my grandma and grandpa's house and talk to them. Maybe they can help." Since we were too young to drive, we started off on a two- or three-mile hike through winding hills and neighborhoods.

It was around six o'clock and still light when we arrived. I clearly remember Dewey's grandmother greeting us at the front door and graciously inviting us into their warm and cozy "old people's home" (that's how I viewed it, anyway). We plopped down on the comfortable couch in the living room, and Grandma brought us lemonade and cookies. Then she and Grandpa sat down with us. Dewey's grandfather settled into his chair and talked with us about nothing in particular. We were just shooting the breeze until Dewey and I got to the point of our visit.

Grandma and Grandpa must have been a little taken aback when Dewey suddenly asked, "Who is Jesus Christ?" They must have been more surprised when I followed up with a stream of "lightweight" questions: "What is the Bible about? Does prayer work? Is there a heaven? If so, did Dewey's mom and my brother go to heaven? And what about hell—is that real?"

A quaint little after-dinner visit became shaded in serious tones. Those kind, gracious Christian people were touched by our innocent inquiries concerning spiritual things. They patiently listened as we shared some of our thoughts and struggles. Looking back through the telescope of time, I can scarcely recall the explanations they offered in response to our queries. But I vividly remember a gesture that "spoke louder than words": Without hesitation, that genial old grandpa reached toward the table next to his chair and took hold of his well-worn

Bible. He opened it, leafed through crinkly pages, and read to us. The husband and wife both answered questions, which meant each of them knew God and the Bible. After we had talked for an hour or two, they prayed with us.

On the trek home in the dark, Dewey and I talked and pondered the truths we had just heard, not knowing that seeds had been planted into both of our young and impressionable hearts. Those seeds would come to fruition in my life about a decade and a half later when I accepted God's love for me. (Unfortunately, I have not been in contact with Dewey for many years, but I pray that the seeds sowed long ago took root in his life as well.)

Why did we go to Dewey's grandparents for the answers about life and death? Because Dewey knew they had respect for the Bible and awe for God. In that time of confusion, grief, and searching in my life, I got a glimpse of what the Bible can do. It provides comfort, it provides wisdom, it provides guidance. It is the first place to go in times of sadness or gladness.

I find it interesting that after all these years, what I remember most clearly is Grandpa reaching for his Bible and leaving it open on his lap as we talked. That gesture spoke volumes: "In this book, you will find all the answers to your deepest questions. You will find healing for your hurts. You will find strength in the midst of your sorrow."

I'm thankful for that early experience—and others like it later on—that instilled in me a love and reverence for the Bible. Although I rejected God and His Word during my many years of wandering, I had the inkling down deep that the Bible was a wonderful treasure. In time, that small stirring would flourish into full-fledged confidence in and love for the Bible.

I hope you will take these words as an encouragement to examine your own paradigm toward the Scriptures. If there is any part of you that sees the Bible as an obligation and requirement, I ask you to turn your thinking around. The Holy Bible is truly a privilege to enjoy, a gift to savor.

Chapter Four

Check the Directions

The Bible Is Our "Owner's Manual" for a Great Life

When we find ourselves deficient in wisdom, it is not because the Word of God has pages missing, but because we have not seen all there is on the pages we already have. It is not more knowledge we require, but better vision to see what has already been revealed in Jesus Christ.

Eugene Peterson

Have you ever tried to figure out the remote control for your television set? I find myself calling our cable company at least once or twice a year to say, "Hey, how do I make this thing work?"

Inevitably, some techie on the other end of the line asks, "Well, Mister MacIntosh, did you read the instruction manual?"

You're probably like me—you either can't bring yourself to actually read an owner's manual or you can't decipher the hieroglyphics if you do read it. There is probably nothing more irritating than a manual for whatever gadget, gizmo, or appliance you might have.

During my research, I discovered one group of professionals that apparently isn't into owner's manuals. A sign in an engineering firm's reception area read: "Real engineers don't read owner's manuals. Reliance on a reference book is a hallmark of the novice and the coward." Another wall held the following sign: "Real engineers don't seek technical support. To do so is a sign of weakness."

Engineers are probably the only ones in our society who can comprehend gadgets and devices without some kind of manual. The rest of us need help to figure out all the buttons, blinking lights, and electronics that overwhelm us.

As frustrated as we might become with electronic devices, there's something far more important we need help with: our lives and the problems we face, the challenges we encounter, and the sorrows we endure. Since we are created beings with a free will and a purpose for our lives, there must be some instructions for us somewhere that ensure we will function at optimal capacity. I would like to suggest that the Bible is just such a book, put here so you and I can live up to our maximum potential. In fact, if I were given the assignment of coming up with a new title for the Bible, it might very well be:

LIFE: AN OWNER'S MANUAL
Your Time-Honored, Time-Tested Guide to the
Here and Now
and the
Then and There.

As I said in the last chapter, the Bible is not a stuffy tome full of dos and don'ts. It is bursting with stories, letters, poetry, and practical advice on how to maintain healthy relationships, attain peace of mind, excel in your chosen vocation, find purpose and meaning, and live long and prosper. I agree with author Mark Buchanan, who said:

> *The Bible is not a book of philosophy—deep thoughts to ponder. It is more like a manual. You don't read a book on kayaking technique simply to ponder the idea. You read it to learn how to kayak. ...*
>
> *The book—God-breathed, every word of it—is useful. Useful for what? For propping up overheads? No. For studying the ancient languages and customs and cultures of the Middle East? Well, maybe. But that's not what Paul had in mind. How about for devising and defending certain theological systems? Again, we are wandering off the mark. The Bible is useful for this: shaping and training you to be the kind of person who walks in righteousness and is ready to do good works, God's works, in a fallen world.*[1]

> I WANT TO PARTICIPATE IN GOD'S OUTRAGEOUS PLAN TO LOVE, HELP, AND RESCUE PEOPLE ALL OVER THE WORLD.

Please understand that when I refer to the Bible as an "owner's manual," I am not suggesting that it is only a pragmatic, practical, how-to reference book. It is a sacred, hallowed book replete with mystery and inscrutability. If you are someone who enjoys pondering the complexities of life, death, and eternity, you will find a lifetime's worth of material in the pages of the Holy Scriptures. But all of us, either occasionally or incessantly, need help with the daily, ongoing challenges of life. For any and every issue we might face, the Bible offers wisdom and direction.

WHO NEEDS DIRECTIONS?

It's become a staple of comedians, screenwriters, and joke-tellers everywhere: The exasperated man behind the steering wheel, driving in circles in an unfamiliar area, hopelessly lost. But he refuses to stop for directions, even if his life depended on it. Beside him, his wife rolls her eyes, sighs dramatically, and says for the hundredth time, "For Pete's sake, would you just stop and ask for help!"

FOR ANY AND EVERY ISSUE WE MIGHT FACE, THE BIBLE OFFERS WISDOM AND DIRECTION.

When it comes to the nitty-gritty of our lives—managing finances, raising kids, maintaining relationships—we do need guidance and direction. Why? Because all of us are far from perfect, and every person on earth has shortcomings, weaknesses, and blind spots. There is obviously a major flaw abiding in the human race—a malfunction that keeps us from operating at our full capability. This is a flaw found in the young and old, male and female, Asian or European, Latino or Caucasian, in all peoples on every continent. That flaw is what the Bible calls sin. And sin causes people to live apart from God and mess up their lives in a myriad of ways.

Saint Paul spoke to the Christian community that was living in the "eternal city" of Rome. Known as one of the world's ancient superpowers, Rome was immersed in sinful living. Paul acknowledged that sin causes people to undermine their true potential: "For all have sinned, and come short of the glory of God" (Romans 3:23 KJV).

Since the Bible declares openly that the human race is in a fallen state, we need to turn to someone or something for the answers. The Bible is the one book that can be relied upon to speak the truth, teach the truth, and impart the truth. It is not a sign of weakness or helplessness to seek the Creator's assistance for getting our lives in order. For God, it is a sign of inner strength that His children would seek His "technical assistance."

Human pride is subtle at times, and it can destroy our lives and families without our even knowing that it is working against us. Pride would keep you from seeking the truth under the guise that you are a weakling if you need a crutch like religion and God. On the contrary, God is not my crutch; He is my complete intensive care unit. I cannot make it through one day without Him and His presence in my life.

The Bible will supply specific guidance for any issue we might encounter—if we'll only utilize the owner's manual God has provided for us. Although the Scriptures address literally hundreds of subjects and concerns that humans face, let's highlight just a few that can enable us to lead rich and satisfying lives:

Good Emotional and Mental Health

The Bible is teeming with references to peace, calm, joy, delight, pleasure, rest, solitude, and dozens of similar words. It strikes me that God's book is the greatest reference guide to emotional and mental wellness. I doubt there is anything in the Bible that would be considered mentally unhealthy by the most insightful and complete psychology textbooks. As a matter of fact, Barna Research Group found that:

* ❋ Eighty-two percent of regular Bible readers described themselves as "at peace" compared to 58 percent of those who said they never read the Bible.
* ❋ Seventy-eight percent of regular Bible readers said they felt "happy" all or most of the time compared to 67 percent of nonreaders.
* ❋ Sixty-eight percent of regular Bible readers said they were "full of joy" compared to 44 percent who said they never read the Bible.[2]

Our society is, of course, plagued by emotional difficulties such as depression, anger mismanagement, and anxiety disorders. It's astounding how many people are distraught and distressed. Many of these people find help and healing through therapy, support groups, and books. That's terrific. I believe, however, that the best cure for whatever ails us comes straight from God and His book.

Long before there were schools of psychology, clinics and treatment centers, and programs of every kind, there was the sound, solid truth of the Bible. The principles and guidelines found therein lead us to wholeness and health. For example:

❀ Lower your stress level. "Make it your ambition to lead a quiet life, to mind your own business and to work with your hands, just as we told you, so that your daily life may win the respect of outsiders and so that you will not be dependent on anybody" (1 Thessalonians 4:11–12).

❀ Let go of anxiety. "Do not worry about your life, what you will eat or drink; or about your body, what you will wear. Is not life more important than … clothes? Look at the birds of the air; they do not sow or reap or store away in barns, and yet your heavenly Father feeds them. Are you not much more valuable than they? Who of you by worrying can add a single hour to his life?" (Matthew 6:25–27)

> YOU ARE SIGNIFICANT. YOUR LIFE DOES HAVE MEANING. IT SAYS SO RIGHT THERE IN GOD'S BOOK.

❀ Cultivate harmonious relationships. "If it is possible, as far as it depends on you, live at peace with everyone" (Romans 12:18). "Make every effort to live in peace with all men" (Hebrews 12:14).

❅ Talk about your struggles. "Confess your sins to each other and pray for each other so that you may be healed" (James 5:16).

❅ Find a support system. "Let us consider how to stimulate one another to love and good deeds, not forsaking our own assembling together, as is the habit of some, but encouraging one another" (Hebrews 10:24–25 NASB).

Nearly every psychologist and mental-health professional would affirm that to be tried-and-true advice. We should not be surprised that after many years of studying human behavior, Harvard psychiatrist Robert Coles remarked: "Nothing I have discovered about the makeup of human beings contradicts in any way what I have learned from the Hebrew prophets such as Isaiah, Jeremiah, and Amos, and from the book of Ecclesiastes, and from Jesus and the lives of those He touched. Anything that I can say as a result of my research into human behavior is a mere footnote to those lives in the Old and New Testaments."[3]

The authors of the Bible tell us that a cleansing takes place in our lives when we read the Scriptures. As the psalmist said, "How can a young man cleanse his way? By taking heed according to Your word" (119:9 NKJV). That word *cleanse* also is found in the following passage: "Husbands, love your wives, just as Christ loved the church and gave himself up for her to make her holy, cleansing her by the washing with water through the word" (Ephesians 5:25–26).

God would have us participate in a cleansing regimen. There is no better way for us to clean out all the dirt and debris from our mind, spirit, and soul than to make the Bible a regular part of our daily lives.

A Sense of Profound Significance

Every person on earth desperately wants to feel valued, worthwhile, and important. Yet many men and women wrestle with questions such as: Does my life matter? Is my time on earth going to amount to anything? Does anyone really care about me?

These questions are answered resoundingly by the Scriptures. As the psalmist wrote, "How precious also are thy thoughts unto me, O God! How great is the sum of them! If I should count them, they are more in number than the sand" (139:17–18 KJV). Without a doubt, this is one of my favorite Scriptures. That's because I seem to have negative thoughts about myself. Yet God thinks so highly of me that my sense of significance is bolstered and buttressed again and again.

I came across a government Web site that allows people to ask questions of a scientist. I spotted one query that immediately reminded me of the psalm quoted above: "Are there more stars or are there more grains of sand?" The expert supplied this answer:

> *If every star came with a planet like earth that had billions of sand grains, there would have to be more sand grains than stars! The number of stars in our galaxy is around 100 billion or 10^{11} in exponential notation. The number of sand grains on earth is probably somewhere between 10^{20} and 10^{24}. The number of sand grains on earth is therefore much greater than the number of stars in our galaxy.*

However, our galaxy is only one of about 100 billion in the visible universe, and so the total number of stars we know about is around 10^{22}, which is kind of in the same ballpark as the number of grains of sand on earth. Of course, those numbers are much bigger than we can count.[4]

Wow! It's unbelievable how much God loves us. This is amazing, because when you get anywhere close to fathoming the number of precious thoughts God has for you, you have to cry out like the psalmist, "How great is the sum of them!"

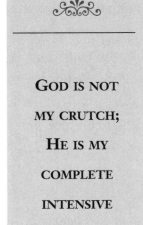

GOD IS NOT MY CRUTCH; HE IS MY COMPLETE INTENSIVE CARE UNIT.

Are you someone who struggles with a sense of meaning in life? Do you wonder if you—being one among billions of people on earth—have value and significance? I struggle with those questions from time to time, and when I do, I open my "owner's manual" and review the psalm above. If I need more reassurance, I read Paul's letter to the Christians living in Rome:

I am convinced that neither death nor life, neither angels nor demons, neither the present nor the future, nor any powers, neither height nor depth, nor anything else in all creation, will be able to separate us from the love of God that is in Christ Jesus our Lord (8:38–39).

You are significant. Your life does have meaning. You are greatly loved. It says so right there in God's book.

Sound Financial Advice

Many people don't consider money a spiritual issue. They consider it a worldly commodity, a necessary evil for survival in day-to-day life. Yet Jesus talked more about money than almost any other topic. He knew that how we handle money is symptomatic of more pervasive issues—such as greed versus generosity, contentment versus avarice, self-sufficiency versus trust in God.

In our modern western culture, of course, there is a massive industry devoted to making money, managing money, and manipulating money. Nearly everyone wants to utilize money wisely. The Bible provides us with sound principles for managing money and, more important, managing our attitude toward money. A few examples:

Stay out of debt. Going into debt obligates us—and in a sense enslaves us—to another person or institution. We limit our flexibility and freedom, and we add anxiety to our lives as we worry about how to pay off credit cards, home equity loans, and all the rest. As the proverb says, "The rich rule over the poor, and the borrower is servant to the lender" (22:7).

Setting aside extra funds is prudent. Having money saved enables us to handle emergencies without going into debt, and it also allows us to share with others out of our surplus (you can't give what you don't have). Keeping some money in reserve makes good sense: "In the house of the wise are stores of choice food and oil, but a foolish man devours all he has" (Proverbs 21:20).

It is better to be industrious than indolent. Sometimes people encounter money trouble due to unfortunate circumstances or unavoidable crises; other times it's due to sheer laziness: "All hard work brings a profit, but mere talk leads only to poverty" (Proverbs 14:23).

Work diligently rather than going after get-rich-quick schemes. There's no end to plans and programs that promise instant wealth. The problem is, most of them do not deliver. Heed this counsel instead: "He who works his land will have abundant food, but the one who chases fantasies will have his fill of poverty" (Proverbs 28:19).

Ultimately, everything we have comes from God. As John pointed out, "A man can receive only what is given him from heaven" (John 3:27). Because God owns everything, we can trust Him to supply what we need: "My God will meet all your needs according to his glorious riches in Christ Jesus" (Philippians 4:19).

The Bible may not give you specific advice about managing your 401(k) or diversifying your portfolio, but it tells you everything you need to attain financial peace of mind. This is the kind of practical, helpful wisdom we find throughout the Bible—wisdom intended to enhance and enrich our lives.

YOUR GUIDE TO ADVENTURE

I have the privilege of talking with many people who are investigating the Christian faith. That is, they are checking it out to see what it's all about and if it's something they want to invest their lives in. Here's what they sometimes say: "Christianity sounds good and helpful—and if it works for you, that's great. But I need adventure and action. I want excitement. I just can't see myself sitting in church all the time, going to Bible classes, or singing hymns every Sunday night."

Somewhere along the line, these people came to believe that the Christian life is synonymous with monastic life—meditating by candlelight for hours on end, chanting sacred songs six times a day, and taking meals in silence. Sometimes I tell these folks about my own experiences: journeys I've made to exotic places to tell about God's love, miracles I've witnessed, amazing people I've met—people every bit as brave and daring as Indiana Jones.

Other times, I simply say: "You really ought to read the Bible. If you want action and adventure, just open God's book and start reading." God wants us to have fulfilling, adventurous lives; His Word tells us how to do that.

One of America's great pastors and Bible teachers was Ray C. Stedman. Ray was a minister who truly believed in studying the Bible and teaching it to his church, Palo Alto Bible Church in Palo Alto, California. For many years he taught a study every Sunday evening under the title of "Adventuring Through the Bible." Pastor Stedman's title for that series was right-on, for adventure is found in many of the stories in Scripture. And excitement is found when we must exercise faith concerning the things we discover there.

If it's adventure and excitement you want out of life, ask God to do something amazing through you. If you're genuinely willing to go where God wants you to go and do what God wants you to do, then get ready for action. Fasten your seat belt—it's going to be a wild ride! Just take a look at some people in the Bible who let God work through their lives. Start by reading Hebrews, chapter 11, where there is a list of men and women whose exploits are more spine-tingling than anything Hollywood could come up with. The writer of Hebrews cuts short his list:

> *I do not have time to tell about [all those] who through faith conquered kingdoms, administered justice, and gained what was promised; who shut the mouths of lions, quenched the fury of the flames, and escaped the edge of the sword; whose weakness was turned to strength; and who became powerful in battle and routed foreign armies. (11:32–34).*

I don't want to live a predictable, humdrum life. I want to participate in God's outrageous plan to love, help, and rescue people all over the world. How about you? I encourage you to open the Bible and see if you don't get caught up in the drama of it all.

FUNCTIONING AS THE AUTHOR PLANNED

Pastor Tim Quinn of Holland, Michigan, faced a challenge. His old Macintosh laptop simply would not run his MacBible software anymore. Though he tinkered and fiddled with it for hours, nothing helped. His wife suggested that he call the owners of the software company for assistance. But no, he kept trying and trying—without success. He tells what happened next:

> *That morning, after having exhausted every last idea, I gave in and called the MacBible Corporation. After speaking to a friendly voice, I was assured that the person to whom I was being referred would know exactly what to do. I wasn't convinced, but I agreed to give it a try.*

The name I had been given sounded familiar, and I soon learned why. The person on the other end of the line was none other than the man who wrote the MacBible software. He gave me a brief set of instructions; I took them down and hung up the phone. In minutes, my computer software program was up and running. I just had to go to the man who wrote the program.[5]

The experience confirmed for Tim precisely what we've been discussing. Tim continued:

How many times in life do we try to work out our problems our own way? Finally, when all else has failed, we go to the one who designed us. If we obey, we find ourselves once again at peace with God and functioning as He planned.

God is indeed the Creator of all things and the author of our owner's manual for healthy, happy living. Join me in checking the directions.

CHAPTER FIVE

YOU ARE NOT ALONE

SCRIPTURE SHOWS US HOW TO HAVE RICH, REWARDING RELATIONSHIPS

The Bible was not given to increase our knowledge
but to change our lives.
D. L. MOODY

I thoroughly enjoy the classic Christmas movie *It's a Wonderful Life,* which celebrates one man's extraordinary generosity. George Bailey, the proprietor of a building and loan institution, demonstrates compassion, hope, and trust in others, even when adversity strikes. The trouble begins when George's absent-minded uncle, Billy, misplaces $8,000. George realizes he could go to jail for his uncle's mistake, and he wishes he'd never been born. He wonders if his life has made any difference.

Then an angel named Clarence Oddbody is dispatched from heaven to show George what the world would have been like had he not been born. George sees that the people's lives would have been much worse if not for his contribution. He discovers that in spite of his financial woes, he is a wealthy man because of the investments he made all his life in those around him.

George then returns to the real world grateful to be alive. Even though the law wants him for the missing $8,000, George is thrilled to know his life has purpose and meaning. As he enters the front door of his home, he sees the bank examiner and the sheriff awaiting him. Eyeing his children, George runs to hug and kiss them. When his wife, Mary, comes through the door, he greets her with a loving embrace.

> WHEN WE JOIN WITH OTHER BELIEVERS IN CHRIST, WE SHARE A COMMON PURPOSE AND MISSION THAT BIND US TOGETHER.

"You have no idea what happened to me," he tells her.

She responds, "You have no idea what happened while you were gone."

Hearing the commotion of an approaching crowd, Mary motions for George to stand in front of the decorated Christmas tree in the living room. Uncle Billy is the first to enter the house, carrying a wicker basket full of cash. He dumps it all on the table in front of George.

"Mary told people you were in trouble, and they scattered all over town collecting money," Billy explains. "They didn't ask any questions. They just wanted to help."

People then fill the living room and pile money on the table. Mr. Martini, owner of the local nightclub, brings money from the jukebox. Mr. Gower, the druggist whom George worked for as a boy, gives all his accounts-receivable funds. Millionaire Sam Wainwright, a lifelong friend, sends a telegram promising to supply whatever balance remains. George's war-hero brother enters and proposes a toast, "To my brother, the richest man in town!"

George spots a book on top of the pile of money. He opens it and discovers it's a gift from Clarence, his guardian angel. The inscription reads, "No man is a failure who has friends."

I am moved by that scene because of the love and affection demonstrated to George by his friends, family, and acquaintances. He doesn't realize how valuable he is to each of them until they all rally around in his moment of need. Suddenly, George understands how blessed he is because of the wonderful folks in his life.

Isn't that what we long for—to be surrounded by people who genuinely love us and care for us? Don't we all want an intimate marriage, dear friends, and a tight-knit social group with whom to share our lives? That's what I want, and I bet you do, too. Let me tell you something: That is the kind of caring community and supportive fellowship described in the Bible.

God created each human being to enjoy companionship and camaraderie with others, and He tells us how to achieve that in the Bible. As the apostle Paul says, "Be devoted to one another in brotherly love. Honor one another above yourselves. ... Be joyful in hope, patient in affliction, faithful in prayer. Share with God's people who are in need" (Romans 12:10, 12–13). The apostle Peter echoed that theme, "Now that you have purified yourselves by obeying the truth so that you have sincere love for your brothers, love one another deeply, from the heart" (1 Peter 1:22).

But it's not always easy, is it? Though we all desire a happy marriage and a gathering of close friends, it doesn't happen very often. This world we live in can be cold and cruel—and it is far from God's ideal. You only have to pick up the local newspaper, and the headlines will shout about human relations gone awry. You only have to hear the latest research report detailing divorce statistics and fractured families to be reminded that relationships are in big trouble.

Yet what is more blissful here on earth than friends getting along? Or belonging to a family who loves each other and works together? Or neighbors who support each other? Most of our lives are spent in relationships, and many of our treasured experiences involve other people. If you were to recount your greatest memories, you would almost certainly realize that they include others.

The Bible is filled with stories of love and hate, friendship and rivalry, unresolved clashes and successful resolution. In order to achieve the rich relationships described in the Scriptures, we have to work hard, pray fervently, and pore over God's instructions so we'll know the best way to act and think. Let's look at three qualities the Bible says are essential for developing healthy, happy relationships. Then, once we've established that foundation, we'll explore the contexts in which we can pursue the most rewarding relationships.

THE HIGH CALLING OF HUMILITY

In our self-centered, me-first society, we don't hear much about humility. Corporations do not proffer bonuses for "The Employee Demonstrating Exemplary Meekness." High school graduations do not include awards for the student "Most Likely to Live a Humble, Unassuming Life." A deferential, self-sacrificing attitude usually goes unnoticed and unrecognized.

Yet this is one of the qualities mentioned repeatedly in the Scriptures. Jesus and many of the biblical writers tell us that humility is critical for promoting harmony and unity in our relationships. As the apostle Paul said: "Do nothing out of selfish ambition or vain conceit, but in humility consider others better than yourselves. Each of you should look not only to your own interests, but also to the interests of others" (Philippians 2:3–4). He goes on to give us the rationale behind his instruction:

> *Your attitude should be the same as that of Christ Jesus: Who, being in very nature God, did not consider equality with God something to be grasped, but made himself nothing, taking the very nature of a servant, being made in human likeness. And being found in appearance as a man, he humbled himself and became obedient to death—even death on a cross (Philippians 2:5–8).*

This is the kind of passage that momentarily takes my breath away. Jesus gave up everything and died a humiliating death for you and me. Our calling is to follow His example of servanthood and self-sacrifice. Though few of us will be called

89

upon to surrender our lives for another person, we can expect regular opportunities to demonstrate unselfishness, kindness, and consideration for others.

I heard about an incident that occurred at Lake Elementary School in Oceanside, California, which is about an hour from where I live. Mr. Alter's fifth-grade class included fourteen boys who were completely bald. Only one, however, had no choice in the matter. Ian O'Gorman, undergoing chemotherapy for lymphoma, faced the prospect of having all his hair fall out in clumps. Rather than enduring that slow indignity, he had his head shaved. Ian was surprised—and no doubt grateful—to find that thirteen of his classmates shaved their heads as well so he wouldn't feel embarrassed and self-conscious.

"If everybody has his head shaved, sometimes people don't know who's who," said eleven-year-old Scott Sebelius. "They don't know who has cancer and who has just shaved their head."

Ten-year-old Kyle Hanslik started it all. He talked to some other boys, and before long they all trekked to the local barbershop. "The last thing [Ian] would want is to not fit in," Kyle said. "We just wanted to make him feel better."[1]

That's humbleness and self-sacrifice in action. What a perfect example of the verse, "In humility consider others more important than yourselves." When we love others, we will make many sacrifices—time, energy, money, and perhaps even our dignity. In doing so, we create deep and meaningful relationships.

FOCUS ON FORGIVENESS

Solomon, one of the wisest people to walk the earth, once wrote, "He who covers over an offense promotes love, but whoever repeats the matter separates close friends" (Proverbs 17:9). If you want to divide a friendship—or any relationship—hold on to every insult issued and wrong committed. If you want to maintain happy relationships, however, learn the art of forgiveness.

Indeed, the whole idea of forgiveness originated with our great and merciful God. It is such an amazing plan that God thought up to get our attention. The plan of salvation through His Son, Jesus, is not something that a religious person could have conceived. It was Jesus who said, "For God so loved the world that He gave His only begotten Son, that whoever believes in Him should not perish but have everlasting life" (John 3:16 NKJV). The death of His Son opened the door for your forgiveness.

> THE BIBLE IS FILLED WITH STORIES OF LOVE AND HATE, FRIENDSHIP AND RIVALRY, UNRESOLVED CLASHES AND SUCCESSFUL RESOLUTION.

Just think if it were you on the cross, after hours of interrogation, whipping, beatings, and deplorable treatment. What would your attitude be not only toward the people torturing you, but also toward the people of the world? Probably it would not be very charitable and loving. But Jesus said, "Father, forgive them, for they do not know what they do" (Luke 23:34 NKJV). He did not make this statement after His baptism. Nor did He say these words at the marriage feast in the small town of Cana. Jesus spoke words of forgiveness while hanging on a cross, with nails in His hands and feet.

With Jesus as our role model, we are encouraged to demonstrate that same attitude: "Bear with each other and forgive each other whatever grievances you may have against one another. Forgive as the Lord forgave you. And over all these virtues put on love, which binds them all together in perfect unity" (Colossians 3:13–14). It is not always easy to forgive everyone—in many cases it is flat-out difficult to do. The apostle Paul understood that because he dealt with people all of the time. His writings and historical record show that people did not always deal kindly with Paul. Yet the love of God allowed him to forgive even those who did him great harm, and he was able to grow from his experiences.

LET LOVE PREVAIL

The apostle John ended his depiction of Jesus' life by saying: "Jesus did many other things as well. If every one of them were written down, I suppose that even the whole world would not have room for the books that would be written" (John 21:25). Fortunately, there are more than enough stories about Jesus (and others) in the New Testament to teach us how to love one another. After all, Jesus loved widows, children, the rich, the poor, military personnel, government workers, the sick, the dying, and the dead. Let's look at one story and see how we can learn about love:

> *Now on his way to Jerusalem, Jesus traveled along*
> *the border between Samaria and Galilee. As he was*
> *going into a village, ten men who had leprosy met him.*
> *They stood at a distance and called out in a loud voice,*
> *"Jesus, Master, have pity on us!"*

*When he saw them, he said, "Go, show yourselves
to the priests." And as they went, they were cleansed.*

*One of them, when he saw he was healed, came
back, praising God in a loud voice. He threw himself at
Jesus' feet and thanked him—and he was a Samaritan.*

*Jesus asked, "Were not all ten cleansed? Where are
the other nine? Was no one found to return and give
praise to God except this foreigner?" Then he said to
him, "Rise and go; your faith has made you well"*
(Luke 17:11–19).

There is no definition in the law concerning the distance a
leper is supposed to stand from a healthy person. One authority said when a leper was windward of a healthy person, he
should stand at least fifty yards away. That shows us the isolation these leprous people lived with. When they stood "at a distance," Jesus responded to their call by telling them to go to the
priests as the law said. On the way, in obedience to His word,
they were cleansed. Imagine the joy of having an illness or serious condition immediately taken from you. How thrilling it
must have been for those ten people to look at their flesh and
see that they were normal once again.

Love appears as Jesus hears the cry of these social rejects. His
compassion is demonstrated to them through His healing word.
Then love comes back to Jesus as one of the ten returned to give
thanks for the love shown. Notice that there are four attributes
of this thankful person: he returned; spoke with a loud voice; fell
down on his face at Jesus' feet; and gave thanks. This is an excellent example of love flowing in both directions. Jesus reached
out to the ailing man and healed him. Recognizing the gift he'd
been given, the man returned to give thanks.

Interestingly, Jesus pointed out the only one to return to give thanks was not a Jew. This "foreigner" reminds us that the grace of God is for all people in all places. The Bible helps us learn how to love, not only in giving love but also in receiving love. Let's not forget that being thankful with a humble heart is a vital part of loving relationships.

YOU CAN HAVE A WONDERFUL MARRIAGE AND FAMILY

Each year, hundreds of self-help books are published in the marriage and family category. Some of these are indeed helpful, while others are decidedly unhelpful. Add to these the dozens of seminars, TV programs, and radio shows dispensing advice for spouses and parents, and you've got lots and lots of information.

> GOD CREATED EACH HUMAN BEING TO ENJOY COMPANIONSHIP AND CAMARADERIE WITH OTHERS, AND HE TELLS US HOW TO ACHIEVE THAT IN HIS BOOK.

Sandy and I have benefited greatly from some books and programs that have strengthened our marriage and improved our parenting skill over the years. But I never fail to be impressed by the single most insightful, practical, inspirational self-help book of all: the Bible. The Scriptures provide sound guidance and time-tested wisdom for our closest relationships. Here's just a sampling:

* "Husbands ought to love their wives as their own bodies. He who loves his wife loves himself. After all, no one ever hated his own body, but he feeds and cares for it, just as Christ does the church" (Ephesians 5:28–29).
* "Marriage should be honored by all, and the marriage bed kept pure, for God will judge the adulterer and all the sexually immoral" (Hebrews 13:4).
* "Fathers, do not exasperate your children; instead, bring them up in the training and instruction of the Lord" (Ephesians 6:4).
* "If anyone does not provide for his relatives, and especially for his immediate family, he has denied the faith and is worse than an unbeliever" (1 Timothy 5:8).
* "Husbands, in the same way be considerate as you live with your wives, and treat them with respect as the weaker partner and as heirs with you of the gracious gift of life" (1 Peter 3:7).

The theme woven throughout all biblical counsel regarding family relations is to treat each other with utmost love, care, respect, and fairness. Although there are psychologists and therapists who are dead-set against the Bible, I wonder if their opinion might change if they actually read the passages related to marriage and parenting. It is hard to argue with a counseling treatment plan based on mutual respect and kindness.

When I fell in love with the Bible as a young Christian man, it was at a time when many of my peers were caught up in drugs and every kind of degradation. My generation was protesting the Vietnam War, chanting "Ban the bomb," and listening to a drugged-out Harvard psychology professor propagating a doctrine of flagrant waste of youth and potential. Dr. Timothy Leary, addled with LSD, sent his mantra to the young men and women of America: "Tune in, turn on, and drop out." Sadly, too many young people followed his ill-conceived advice. America's youth were told that they were "flower children" and they should "make love, not war."

One the most devastating aftermaths of the sixties and seventies was the erosion of the traditional marriage and family structure. Marriage has been decimated over the past half century, resulting in immeasurable collective and individual pain. It does not take an expert to realize that the durability of marriages, as well as the quality of marriages, has plummeted over the past decades.

This is a tragedy because marriage is sacred and sanctified by God. Marriage is about far more than two people combining their household goods, vacationing together, and opening a joint checking account. There is something profoundly spiritual and transcendent when a man and woman commit themselves to each other for life. Marriage involves a covenant between each person and God.

God, the Creator of marriage, views this union as holy and hallowed: "A man will leave his father and mother and be united to his wife, and two will become one flesh. ... Therefore what God has joined together, let man not separate" (Matthew 19:5–6). We must restore to marriage all the importance and value that God intended.

If we as a society want to restore the sacredness and stability of marriage and the family, we need to return to the One who created them. More specifically, if you want to maintain a strong marriage and enjoy a happy family life, begin by embracing the guidance, counsel, and encouragement found in the Word of God. View the Bible as the first and best source of wisdom.

Gerald and Geneva Clark of Spartanburg, South Carolina, have been married since 1944. That's a long and successful marriage. When they were asked the secret of their success, they went right to the Bible. Specifically, they pointed to Jesus' command to "love your neighbor as yourself." They explained: "If you were to ask Jesus, 'Who is my neighbor?' He would tell you that you have many neighbors, the closest of whom is your mate. Be the best of neighbors to your spouse! Treat your partner exactly as you want to be treated—with honor, respect, patience, kindness, humility, forgiveness. God's command to you, His desire for you, can be summed up, in one word: love."[2]

We can take a lesson from these two veterans of marriage. If you want a long, successful marriage, turn first to the Scriptures. Use it as your source of instruction and inspiration. Study it together with your family as a safeguard and support system.

YOU CAN CONNECT TO A CLOSE COMMUNITY

Do you sometimes feel all alone in life? Do you ever feel like you're stranded on the island with nobody to help you? If you are a moviegoer, you might have seen *Cast Away*, in which Tom Hanks plays a FedEx executive named Chuck Noland.

While on a spur-of-the-moment business trip, Chuck narrowly escapes death when the airplane he's traveling in crashes into the ocean. He finds himself marooned, totally alone, on a deserted island. A few things wash up on shore from the plane's cargo hold, including a volleyball. With no one to talk to, Chuck draws a face on the ball and names him after the manufacturer, "Wilson." He says to his new companion, "Hey, you want to hear something funny? My dentist's name is James Spalding."

Months pass, and isolation takes its toll. Chuck realizes that a leather ball is no substitute for real friends offering real companionship. As he is preparing to attempt an escape from the island on a makeshift raft, Chuck sneers to Wilson, "We might just make it. Did that thought ever cross your brain? Well, regardless, I would rather take my chance out there on the ocean than stay here and die on this [stinking] island the rest of my life, talking to a [ridiculous] volleyball!"

Perhaps you sometimes feel that isolated and desperate. The Devil is an expert at making you feel alone, as if you were on a deserted island. He would like you to feel cut off and distant from other people so you might pursue the wrong crowd or the wrong diversions to assuage your loneliness. Don't buy into it. The "Wilsons" of this world—all the convenient substitutes for loving relationships—can't help us in the long run.

It's not only Satan who tries to make you feel lonely—our culture is a culprit too. Nowadays, we must be intentional about forming and maintaining relationships, because so much about our society encourages isolation. As journalist Laura Pappano says in her book *The Connection Gap: Why Americans Feel So Alone*:

> *People talk a great deal about "community" but complain of feeling less and less a part of one. People long for rich relationships but find themselves wary of committing to others. Many of us hunger for intimacy*

but end up paying professionals to listen to, care for, and
befriend us. ...

As a society, we face a collective loneliness, an empty
feeling that comes not from lack of all human interac-
tion, but from the loss of meaningful interaction, the
failure to be a part of something real, or to have faith
in institutions that might bring us together. [3]

Loneliness may be the single greatest cause of emotional, physical, and spiritual maladies in our society. Yet God never intended it to be this way. He wants each of us to enjoy a rich and rewarding life, and he knows that doing so means authentic and ongoing connection to other people. Compare our culture to the snapshot of the early Christian community we're presented with in God's Word:

All the believers were together and had everything
in common. Selling their possessions and goods, they
gave to anyone as he has need. Every day they contin-
ued to meet together in the temple courts. They broke
bread in their homes and ate together with glad and
sincere hearts, praising God and enjoying the favor of
all the people (Acts 2:44–47).

All the believers were one in heart and mind. No
one claimed that any of his possessions was his own,
but they shared everything they had. ... There were
no needy persons among them. For from time to time
those who owned lands or houses sold them, brought
the money from the sales and put it at the apostles'
feet, and it was distributed to anyone as he had need
(Acts 4:32, 34–35).

> LONELINESS MAY
> BE THE SINGLE
> GREATEST CAUSE
> OF EMOTIONAL,
> PHYSICAL, AND
> SPIRITUAL
> MALADIES IN OUR
> SOCIETY.

Imagine that kind of community, where the people are "one in heart and mind" and there are "no needy persons among them." The church of the twenty-first century is not perfect, and we certainly have our share of problems. But I still believe it is the best place to develop a sense of community and belonging. This is the place we can genuinely know others and be known. When we join with other believers in Christ, we share a common purpose and mission that bind us together.

The writer of Hebrews understood the importance of community: "Let us consider how we may spur one another on toward love and good deeds. Let us not give up meeting together, as some are in the habit of doing, but let us encourage one another" (10:24–25). If you're already involved in a church, home fellowship, Bible study class, or some other group, I encourage you to deepen the bonds. If you have no such group, make it a top priority to find a healthy, devoted "family" to join.

YOU CAN DEVELOP GREAT FRIENDSHIPS

One of the most beautiful examples of close friendship in all of literature—indeed, in human history—features Jonathan and

David, the shepherd boy who became king of Israel. Jonathan was the son of King Saul, a man who was paranoid and greatly threatened by David, suspecting that the lad would one day occupy the throne. You can see how this triangle might become complicated and convoluted—and it certainly did. But despite Saul's attempt to divide the two younger men, they became the best of friends. We read, "Jonathan became one in spirit with David, and he loved him as himself" (1 Samuel 18:1).

If you want to learn how to develop close friendships, read about David and Jonathan in the book of 1 Samuel (see especially chapters 16–20). Or study the relationship between Paul and Barnabas in the book of Acts and other references in Paul's letters. Or look carefully at the book of Ruth, which is filled with examples of close, trusting friendships.

If it's practical suggestions you want, you'll find plenty scattered throughout the Bible. Make it your mission to find passages that talk about friendship, and then meditate on them. For instance:

- ❋ "A friend loves at all times, and a brother is born for adversity" (Proverbs 17:17).
- ❋ "Wounds from a friend can be trusted, but an enemy multiplies kisses" (Proverbs 27:6).
- ❋ "Two are better than one, because they have a good return for their work: If one falls down, his friend can help him up. But pity the man who falls and has no one to help him up!" (Ecclesiastes 4:9–10).

Friendship is one of God's greatest gifts to mankind, and He has provided all the information we need to become "one in spirit" with another individual.

In the book *Stories for the Journey,* William R. White tells about a European seminary professor named Hans and his wife, Enid. World War II forced them to flee to America, where Hans found a job teaching at a seminary. He was warm, gentle, beloved by his students, and he brought Scripture to life for them.

Hans and Enid were very much in love. Nearly every day they took long walks together, holding hands, and they always sat close in church. Everyone who knew them admired their devoted, intimate relationship.

As time passed, Enid died unexpectedly, leaving Hans devastated and overwhelmed with sorrow. Worried because he wouldn't eat or take walks, the seminary president, along with three other friends, visited Hans regularly. But he remained grief-stricken and deeply depressed. Experiencing the dark night of the soul, Hans told his friends, "I am no longer able to pray to God. In fact, I am not certain I believe in God any more."

After a moment of silence, the seminary president said, "Then we will believe for you. We will make your confession for you. We will pray for you." So the four men met daily for prayer, asking God to restore the gift of faith to their dear friend.

Many months later, as they gathered with Hans, he smiled and said, "It is no longer necessary for you to pray for me. Today, I would like you to pray with me." The dark night of the soul had passed. His faith had been restored, due largely to the love and loyalty of his friends. Instead of carrying Hans to Jesus on a stretcher, they had carried him on their prayers.[4]

That is the kind of reward that comes to those who join the community of Christ followers and develop the meaningful relationships described in the Bible. I strive to be someone like those who cared for Hans so genuinely and so tangibly. When we look at the example of Jesus and absorb the message woven throughout the Bible, we too can create the kind of relationships God desires for us. Our marriage can be closer, our friendships richer, and our social network tighter. That is a prize worth pursuing.

CHAPTER SIX

WHAT'S YOUR STORY?

THROUGH ITS VIVID STORIES AND ECLECTIC CHARACTERS, THE BIBLE ALLOWS
US TO BECOME PART OF THE UNFOLDING DRAMA

*When you read God's Word, you must constantly be
saying to yourself, It is talking to me and about me.*
SØREN KIERKEGAARD

Think back on your childhood for a moment. What were
your favorite stories, the tales that fueled your imagination and
filled your mind with vivid images? Perhaps you loved fables
about gallant knights who battled fire-breathing dragons. Or
maybe you enjoyed stories about lovely princesses who find
true love. It could be that you relished stories set on the battle-
field or the ball field, in a castle or a cottage, in a faraway land
or Never-Never Land.

As for me, I enjoyed stories about heroes and sports figures, such as the most decorated U.S. soldier of World War II, Audie Murphy, and the All-American athlete Jim Thorpe. Real-life stories captured my young attention and encouraged me to be a cut above the crowd.

In every country, children grow up listening to fables, bedtime stories, and nursery rhymes. Stories of a cow jumping over the moon or a large egg falling off a wall have captured the imagination of multitudes. Countless stories in countless languages have been painting scenes with the stroke and brush of words.

Centuries ago, Jewish children grew up with the stories of their heritage and the influence of the God of Israel. Handed down through oral tradition, these accounts were remembered and relayed from one generation to the next. The stories featured larger-than-life characters such as Adam and Eve, Cain and Abel, Noah, Queen Esther, Abraham, Isaac and Jacob, and Moses. These were names well-known by the youngest of each clan. The illustrious prophet Elijah must have stood out to those eager minds as a giant of a man, not to mention the literal giant Goliath, mean and nasty— and defeated by a young shepherd named David. Story after story was told and is still being told in synagogues, schools, and homes throughout the world. These time-honored tales have changed and shaped the lives of people from the Jewish heritage and other backgrounds as well.

Since nearly every person on earth loves a good story, don't you find it fascinating that God uses stories to give us insight into the spiritual realm? Jesus loved to tell stories in the form of parables. Jesus used stories to help those who wanted to understand the things of God. Many of the stories Jesus told the crowds shed light upon the nation of Israel and

> **WE SHARE THE STRUGGLES OF THOSE AROUND US TODAY, AND WE CAN RELATE TO THE CHALLENGES FACED BY THOSE WE READ ABOUT IN THE BIBLE.**

the individuals around Him. They dealt with weddings, farming, nature, culture clashes, family dramas, and working-class struggles. His stories were uncomplicated, accessible, and understandable to all of His listeners, be they rich or poor, scholars or uneducated.

To get His points across, Jesus could have distributed syllabi, passed around handouts, and published a workbook with fill-in-the-blank questions. He could have just stood up and lectured, which He did on occasion. But clearly His preferred method of telling people about God's love and holy living was to weave an intriguing tale, then drive home the point.

SEEING OURSELVES IN
THE CONTOURS OF THE BIBLE

Speaking of storytellers, my pastor Chuck Smith is a great one. He knows how to develop and deliver a story with skill. It is this gift that makes him such an effective Bible teacher, for he inspires listeners to use their minds and to look beyond the obvious.

When I was a young Christian and heading into full-time ministry, I learned under Chuck's tutelage as an intern at his church. Chuck's friend and associate pastor LaVerne Romaine was assigned to look after the first group of intern pastors at Calvary Chapel in Costa Mesa, California. That meant he was supposed to keep us from doing something really dumb. So Don McClure, Tom Stipe, and I diligently sat in the front pews of the sanctuary for our weekly one-hour seminar on what to do and what not to do. LaVerne lectured us on how to teach Bible classes, how to solve problems that might arise, how to start new programs, and lots of other crucial topics for wannabe pastors. Frankly, it was always a bit disappointing because Don, Tom, and I had usually spent the entire previous week doing all that we found out we shouldn't be doing.

Romaine (as he was called) was a retired sergeant major with the United States Marine Corps. If you are not familiar with military rank, you should know that being a sergeant major in the armed forces is one of the highest ranks any enlisted personnel can reach. Sergeant major in the USMC carries with it great respect and honor. For me—as a young minister-in-training and a graduate of army basic training—those intern meetings with Romaine were like being scrutinized by a drill sergeant on the parade grounds.

After Pastor Romaine finished barking instructions and reminding us that we weren't even privates in God's army, he would mellow just enough to appear civilian, and he would relax enough so we could talk together. In one of those rare moments when I felt comfortable enough to quiz him, I said, "Romaine, will the day ever come when I'll have read the Bible enough that a picture will begin to develop in my mind that lets me view Genesis to Revelation?" Remember, it was thirty-three years ago that I asked the question. I had been a Christian for two years, and I'd been reading the Bible nonstop all twenty-four months.

This man with the steely demeanor and heart of gold responded, "Mike, when you begin to understand the Bible, it will be like seeing a mountain range with its peaks and valleys. Just as you are enjoying the peaks, you will begin the journey back down into the valleys. Then when you are in the valley, you will enjoy climbing to the next peak to see life from a higher vantage point."

At the time, I thought, *Uh, yeah, okay. I think I know what you mean.* Now—after thirty some years of seasoning—I know exactly what he meant. As my walk with Jesus develops, it seems that where I am in my spiritual growth parallels where I am in my daily Bible reading and learning. The process is as Romaine described, filled with peaks and valleys—but each new insight or understanding takes me to a slightly higher peak.

Keep that in mind as I tell you about a recent incident involving peaks and valleys—the real kind. My good friend Dennis Magnuson took me with him and a few other friends on a mountain-climbing expedition. We challenged Mount Whitney, the tallest mountain in the continental United States. More accurately, it challenged us. At 14,494 feet above sea level, this beautiful mountain takes its toll on even veteran hikers. Warnings abound to seek shelter immediately if storms appear, since many hikers have been killed by lightning strikes.

The time required for the hike is, of course, dependent upon the physical condition of the hiker. Our team allowed three days, with overnight camping on the way up. On the third day, we ascended the summit, and the final three hours were precarious to say the least. Clambering along a narrow ridge, a rock I was holding slipped from my hand and plunged down the steep mountainside. The thought suddenly struck me: *What am I doing here?!* That thought was quickly followed by, *You only get one mistake at this altitude.* This was my first major mountain-climbing experience—and one that my mind and body would not soon forget.

> WE ARE PARTICIPATING IN SOMETHING BIGGER THAN OURSELVES, AND EVERY ONE OF OUR ACTIONS HELPS TO "WRITE" THE ETERNAL STORY.

When I reached a plateau and my anxiety subsided, it became evident what a wimp I am. As I stood sucking in air, I saw two women in their early twenties crossing a snowfield in front of me. As they hiked, they leaned into the mountain since there was a 4,000-foot free fall if they ventured out too far. Then I noticed they were making the return trip very carefully on the trail by placing their feet in footprints created on their initial trek.

When they got close, I asked them, "Why are you coming back this way?"

"Oh, our boyfriends had us carry their backpacks to the summit since they are coming up the other side of the mountain," one of the girls said. "We just took their packs to the summit and we're headed down about 500 feet by your camp to pick up our packs."

Great! That's just what I needed to hear. I had been complaining about how I'd make it the last 650 feet to the top, and these young ladies had been up once with 60-pound backpacks and were going to retrieve the other 60-pound packs. I didn't mention to these ladies that I left my own pack down at the camp because it was too heavy to lug the rest of the way.

Once I reached the summit, the aches and pains shooting through my body were instantly forgotten because of the breathtaking view of the Sierra Nevadas. The sky was clear, visibility unlimited, and the colors more vivid than a high-pixel plasma screen. Absolutely awesome!

You have probably already guessed that going down Mount Whitney was much easier than the strenuous climb up. When we arrived back at our cars, I stood looking up at something that was a challenge to me just three days earlier. I had achieved my dream of reaching the top.

While standing at the summit, I recalled Pastor Romaine's comment about peaks and valleys. Here is the irony of standing on the highest pinnacle of the "lower forty-eight" states. Less than one hundred miles from Mount Whitney is the lowest point in the United States. Death Valley is 262 feet below sea level. Day in and day out, Mount Whitney looms over the lowest place in the country.

This is similar to the Christian walk. God is on the throne of grace and He is watching you day in and day out as you continue your journey through life. For those who genuinely seek God, it is an upward climb. You can look back to see how far you've come. Each story, parable, and episode recorded in the Scriptures is for our benefit and keeps us moving forward. Every thought and insight you get while reading the Bible draws you closer and closer to the one who made you.

Psalm 23 is much like a "Death Valley," for this is where we read, "Yea, though I walk through the valley of the shadow of death, I will fear no evil." And the Bible also has the Mount Whitney summit verse for us in Isaiah 6:1 NKJV, "I saw the Lord sitting on a throne, high and lifted up." It is amazing to think the Bible relates to the valley experiences of our lives as well as the mountaintop experiences. There is the God of love sitting "high and lifted up" above everything, caring for every second of your life, concerned with each breath, willing and able to interact with you at a moment's notice. God is a loving Father and generous King who wants to speak to you through the stories contained in His book.

Like the mountain peaks and valleys, life is an unfolding mystery. From the time of Creation until today, the drama of living is fresh and new every morning. Knowing that you are someone special in God's marvelous plan is exhilarating. Knowing that you have only one life to live and only one life to give opens up new vistas of learning and living.

SEEING OUR REFLECTION IN STORIES

The respected educator and Bible teacher Haddon Robinson emphasizes how biblical characters, with all their adventures and misadventures, serve as a reflection of our own setbacks and successes, tragedies and triumphs. He likens this process to holding up a baby in front of a mirror. When the child moves, the reflection moves. When the baby waves, the reflection waves. Usually, there is that "Aha" moment when the baby's face lights up with understanding. The child suddenly realizes, Hey, that's me!

Dr. Robinson concludes, "Every so often that happens when you're reading the Bible. You pick it up, and it's black print on a white page, telling stories about the long ago and far away. But as you read the text, the print seems to disappear. On the page of Scripture, you see a reflection of yourself."

The Bible presents not only historical accounts and theological concepts, but also dozens of stories that hold up a mirror to us. We can see ourselves in the frightened and weak-kneed Jonah, who did the exact opposite of what God instructed him to do. We can see ourselves in the skeptical Sarah, who burst out laughing when God told her she would have a son in her beyond ripe old age. We see ourselves in the Prodigal Son, rebellious and recalcitrant, finally returning home to a gracious father. When we see ourselves in these people, we can try to emulate their achievements and learn from their failings.

For instance, I realized many years ago that problems can make me either bitter or make me better as a human being. Pastor Chuck pointed out to me one day that the difference between bitter and better is the letter *I*. How interesting that "I" can cause "me" more problems than the crisis I find myself immersed in. If I give myself over to bitterness, it can slow and impede my Christian walk. If in truth my decision is to get better and to be better, then the Holy Spirit can do wonders in and through me.

On Wednesday evenings our church has a gathering, a learning time, called C & V, which stands for Chapter and Verse. Every few years, we start at the very beginning of the Bible, Genesis 1:1, and study through until the last word of Revelation 22:21. I enjoy teaching the Bible because it keeps me spiritually fresh and alert. This morning as I began to work on writing this chapter, I received an e-mail from my friend Stuart, who is an attorney in San Diego. Stuart thanked me for the Bible study on Job from the evening before. He told me he'd noticed something he hadn't seen before—that Job's wife lost ten children in one day just as her husband did, but the two of them responded quite differently. Job chose to worship God and learn from the situation. Job's wife chose to get bitter. She told her husband, "Curse God and die" (Job 2:9).

I had not made that point while teaching about Job, but Stuart had zeroed in on it. That is what's so wonderful about the Bible—everyone can hear and see things from God. Being consumed studying the life of Job, I focused on him and the lessons of his life. Meanwhile, Stuart gained insight from the precautionary tale of Mrs. Job.

Here is some good news about the Bible for you to consider: Just about every situation you find yourself in, the Bible addresses your need or desire. Often we feel isolated and lonely in our struggles. We may think we're going through something that not one other person on earth could identify with. Listen to what the apostle Paul has to say about that:

> *No temptation has overtaken you except such as is*
> *common to man; but God is faithful, who will not allow*
> *you to be tempted beyond what you are able, but with*
> *the temptation will also make the way of escape, that*
> *you may be able to bear it (1 Corinthians 10:13 NKJV).*

I love the phrase "common to man." When it comes to temptation, everyone is pretty much the same. We're in this together! We share the struggles of those around us today, and we can relate to the challenges faced by those we read about in the Bible. Though they lived thousands of years ago, we can learn from the example they set for us. As author Daniel Taylor said, "Stories tell us who we are, why we are here, and what we are to do. They give us our best answers to all of life's big questions, and to most of the small ones as well."[1]

WALKING IN THE FOOTSTEPS OF GIANTS

When I was a teenager, I loved to run. When track season came with the spring, I would sign up and sprint my skinny little legs off. I probably looked like the lead character in Tom Hanks' movie *Forrest Gump*, especially when he's dashing down the field and some-one yells, "Run, Forrest! Run!" I loved running fast, and I had the most fun with sprints and relay teams. Though I wasn't a speedster who would set records or win scholarships, I did love running for the pure joy of it.

GOD IS A LOVING FATHER WHO WANTS TO SPEAK TO YOU THROUGH THE STORIES CONTAINED IN HIS BOOK.

During those high school years, one of my heroes was Rafer Johnson, the amazing track star who won the silver metal in the grueling ten-event decathlon at the 1956 Olympic Games in Rome. Four years later he would triumph and win the gold medal for the same event.

Rafer went to college at UCLA, where he became the first African American to be accepted into a prominent Jewish fraternity. He was president of the UCLA student body his senior year. He came from a very poor family—in fact, after moving to Kingsburg, California, from a small town in Texas, Rafer's family lived in a train boxcar for a time.

He set so many track and field records as a young man that he is considered by most enthusiasts to be among the best all-around track athletes in history. When my friends and I talked about track or read the latest stories about Rafer's feats, it would inspire me to work harder and dream bigger. He motivated me to set my goals higher—and make the effort to achieve them. I was greatly inspired by Rafer, especially knowing of his humble upbringing and how hard he worked to reach his potential.

If you've ever had a hero you admired from afar, you'll love the rest of this story: Years later, Rafer married my wife's best friend, Betsy. She became our oldest son's godmother, and Rafer and I developed a good friendship. He is a great man, whom I've been blessed to know for many years now. I'm very fortunate. It isn't often that we get to meet our heroes, let alone become friends with them.

All of us need heroes, people we can look up to, admire, and seek to emulate. You may have someone you consider a role model—a public figure, a former teacher, a family member. Let me suggest another place to find an example to follow: the pages of the Bible. In the book of Hebrews, chapter 11, we read about fifteen people who are admired both by God and by mankind because of their faith. Set aside some time to look at the characters one by one. Then read firsthand about each one over the coming days and weeks. Use their lives as an example for yourself. Keep a pen or pencil with a notepad next to your Bible, and then write down the things about each person that you relate to. If none of the individuals mentioned in Hebrews 11 sparks your interest as a role model, search the Scriptures until you find someone who does.

Two Old Testament characters in particular helped shape

my early growth as a Christian. Both Elijah and Jeremiah spoke to me about faith and service. Elijah taught me to always trust God and stay faithful to the call on my life. Elijah was a person who seemed to have a special relationship with God. Elijah lived during a time of decadence in Israel, and he was a spokesperson for God to the king and queen. Though they hated him and wanted him dead, he continued to proclaim God's words to them. (If you have never read the biblical account of this amazing man, you can find his story starting in 1 Kings 17.)

I gleaned several lifelong lessons from Elijah's story, especially when the famine came upon the land. God had told Elijah to go to a small brook named Cherith, which seems such an insignificant stream and a place of no prominence. Yet while the drought got worse, God provided fresh water in this remote place. When food was scarce, God had ravens bring Elijah nourishment in the morning and the evening. That story has been with me since the first time I read it many years ago. It taught me then, as it teaches me now, to always go where God leads. Pastor Chuck always says, "Where God guides, God provides." The second lesson I learned from Elijah's obedience was that God can provide for me in supernatural ways. I never have to look to man for provision, but to trust God to supply all I need.

The third lesson I learned from Elijah's story is when God finally dried up the little brook, it was time for Elijah to move on and complete God's call in his life. This shows me how to be sensitive to my surroundings and God's leading. When the provision is no longer there, when the "brook is dried up," it's probably time to move on.

Jeremiah has been a role model because of his calling from

God. In the first chapter of Jeremiah, we learn that he was a young man; in fact, he called himself a "youth." Jeremiah was reluctant to do the work of a prophet and step into a big, important job. He didn't think he had what it took. Yet God told Jeremiah that He had created him and prepared him for such a task.

This encouragement built confidence into me. I never had much self-confidence growing up, and I could easily identify with Jeremiah and his hesitancy to tackle something he couldn't understand or manage. As I read chapter after chapter of the book of Jeremiah, I began to realize the truth: God is strong in our weakness.

Every character in the Bible is there to help you grow closer to God. I encourage you to choose your own favorite characters, people you can identity with, and learn as much as you can from them. As you fall in love with the Bible and all its wonderful characters, you'll grow into the person God intends you to be.

YOU ARE PART OF GOD'S UNFOLDING DRAMA

You might think of the Bible as a compilation of compelling stories, a series of character studies involving people both wicked and wonderful, and a collection of morality tales—parables and real-life episodes that illuminate hidden truths. All of that is certainly true. But if we leave it at that—the Bible as an awe-inspiring anthology—we miss perhaps the most important aspect of all. Scripture is really the story of God, who created people and loved them enough to rescue them and win them to back with His love and grace. It is this story that began at Creation, continues today, and will keep on spreading out into the future. The point is that you are contributing to the story that unfolds and unfurls like a ribbon in time.

Because the Bible tells a story that hasn't finished yet, Christians have a featured part to play, whether they realize it or not. The writer Frederick Buechner describes this story that we find ourselves in:

> *It is a world of magic and mystery, of deep darkness and flickering starlight. It is a world where terrible things happen and wonderful things too. It is a world where goodness is pitted against evil, love against hate, order against chaos, in a great struggle where often it is hard to be sure who belongs to which side because appearances are endlessly deceptive. Yet for all its confusion and wildness, it is a world where the battle goes ultimately to the good, who live happily ever after. ...*
>
> *That is the fairy tale of the Gospel with, of course, one crucial difference from all other fairy tales, which is that the claim made for it is that it is true, that it not only happened once upon a time but has kept on happening ever since and is happening still.*[2]

> EACH STORY, PARABLE, AND EPISODE RECORDED IN THE SCRIPTURES IS FOR OUR BENEFIT AND KEEPS US MOVING FORWARD.

This story we are participating in is true and real, just like every person and every event in the Bible is true and real. You may feel that the part you're playing is insignificant and inconsequential compared to the people you see around you. When you look at others, you may think they're doing more and doing better. I suppose that's only natural in our celebrity-driven culture, where most people clamor for their "fifteen minutes of fame." God does not call any of us to be famous or popular or prominent. In fact, He asks you to fill your unique role with humility, gentleness, and love. One time Jesus told His followers, "If anyone wants to be first, he must be the very last—the servant of all." And, "For he who is least among you all—he is the greatest" (Mark 9:35; Luke 9:48). You do not need to pursue a starring role in God's story; in fact, supporting roles are the most valuable of all.

Seeing our lives in this context should influence the way we think and act and plan. Being part of the "divine drama," as author Kurt Bruner calls it, affords us a profound sense of meaning and value. As Bruner explains:

> *If God is writing and directing an epic drama in which our lives play a part, shouldn't he at least let us in on it? In truth, that is precisely what he has done in the Scriptures. ... What we don't know is how every scene of every subplot in this drama will unfold or how our parts impact the rest of the story. We call that mystery. It's this sense of mystery that turns our daily experiences and choices into a great adventure. The realization and awareness of this adventure infuses with meaning every circumstance we face, every encounter we have, and every decision we make.*

It places us smack in the middle of something bigger than ourselves. ...

Once we've read the script, understanding the larger story, we're better able to grasp and reflect upon where and how our role fits. This infuses every moment of life with new meaning.[3]

How true! We are all participating in something bigger than ourselves, and every one of our actions helps to write the eternal story.

In her book *Mystery on the Desert,* Maria Reiche describes a series of strange lines made by the Nazca in the plains of Peru, some of them covering many square miles. For years, people assumed these lines were the remnants of ancient irrigation ditches. Then in 1939, Dr. Paul Kosok of Long Island University discovered their true meaning could only be seen from high in the air. When viewed from an airplane, these seemingly random lines form enormous drawings of birds, insects, and animals.[4]

Similarly, people often think of the Bible as a series of separate, unrelated stories. When we view the Scriptures as a whole, however, we discover that they form one great story of redemption—from the first "In the Beginning" of Genesis to the final "Amen" of Revelation. Weaving through all the diverse strands of the Bible is a divine story line, the overarching story of how God has rescued, redeemed, and restored fallen human beings, from the first nanosecond of creation through the final cry of victory at the end of time.

CHAPTER SEVEN

FORTIFY YOUR FAITH

THE BIBLE TEACHES US TO LIVE WITH CONFIDENCE AND ASSURANCE

Nobody ever outgrows Scripture.
The book widens and deepens with our years.
CHARLES SPURGEON

On December 17, 2003, the one hundredth anniversary of the Wright brothers' first flight, pilot Brian Binnie was launched in a newly designed rocket—SpaceShipOne—from another aircraft called the White Knight. As the first nongovernment-funded spacecraft of its time, SpaceShipOne's midair launch took place 48,000 feet above sea level. Inside the craft, Binnie flipped a switch that started the jet engine, and in a phenomenal nine seconds, he was in a 60-degree climb and moving heavenward at a speed of 930 miles per hour. Approximately six seconds later when the aircraft reached 68,000 feet, the engine shut off and the craft began its descent to the desert floor below.

Binnie's test flight was cut short, but it still set an astonishing record: That day, SpaceShipOne became the first privately manned aircraft to reach that astounding altitude. Do you think Wilbur and Orville Wright could have ever imagined something of this magnitude? For the Wright brothers, flying just a few feet off of the ground in a straight and level path for less than a hundred yards was enough to fulfill all of their dreams. One hundred years makes a huge difference in technology, doesn't it?

For the designers, builders, and pilot of this experimental aircraft, it took faith to launch the rocket ship for the first time. Teams of enthusiasts took risks and made commitments of time, money, efforts, education, and abilities. Like the Wrights a century before, they all had to exercise faith to realize their goals and accomplish their mission.

CONFIDENCE TO CARRY ON

To varying degrees, life requires faith from all of us. Though few of us will have a chance to—or even want to—fly an untested aircraft, our trust is still put to the test daily. When we see a stoplight turn green and proceed through an intersection, we have faith that other drivers will stop. When we put our trash cans by the curb each week, we trust the garbage collector will remove our rubbish. When we deposit a paycheck, we trust that our employer has the funds available to cover our check. Here in California, we trust that buildings have been engineered so they won't collapse during an earthquake. Obviously, the higher the stakes, the more faith is required.

That's why spiritual faith is so important. Spiritual issues have everything to do with our eternal destination, the quality of our lives here on earth, and our sense of purpose and meaning in life. The most significant aspects of our lives are rooted in spiritual pursuits. Therefore, one of the greatest reasons to fall in love with the Bible is this: It is our source of faith. Indeed, faith is one of the central themes of the Bible. Through stories and written prayers, God's

THE BIBLE IS AN "ADAPTER" THAT PLUGS US IN TO GOD'S POWER AND HELPS US TO GENERATE FAITH.

Word offers encouragement, insight into His character, and examples of how to have an authentic relationship with Him—all elements designed to build up our faith. One of my favorite verses in the New Testament speaks directly to this: "And without faith it is impossible to please God, because anyone who comes to him must believe that he exists and that he rewards those who earnestly seek him" (Hebrews 11:6). This is the type of faith that you and I need to develop in our lives.

Fortunately, all of us have access to faith—God makes it available to everyone! The apostle Paul addresses this in his letter to the Romans: "For by the grace given me I say to every one of you: Do not think of yourself more highly than you ought, but rather think of yourself with sober judgment, in accordance with the measure of *faith* God has given you" (12:3).

I see the Bible as a sort of adapter that plugs us in to God's power and helps us to generate faith. If you have ever traveled internationally, you know that not all wall sockets are created equal. Try plugging your American-made hair dryer or laptop computer into the wall at a German hotel, and you'll see what I mean. I can remember arriving in Europe on one of my first trips abroad and trying to plug my electric shaver into the bathroom wall outlet. To my shock (perhaps *surprise* would be a better word), it didn't work. I was frustrated, but all I really needed was a device called an adapter. This small piece of equipment makes the power accessible, and the adapter allows the appliance to function.

Like an appliance adapter, the Holy Spirit can make the power of heaven available for you, while the Bible can act like an adapter to help you understand God through the culture you live in. Scripture translates God's will into your heart and allows you to follow His commandments and live a life that is pleasing to Him.

I am assuming that you are a seeker of God—the fact that you are reading this book is a good indication that you are hungry to know more about Him. My prayer is that you will enjoy reading the Bible and grow in faith at the same time. Learning this was a life-changing experience for me. During the 1960s, I spent several earnest years searching for God and the meaning of life. My journey led to meditation, yoga, burning incense, spending nights chanting in the desert (in the full pretzel position), practicing my mantra, and reading the life stories of gurus and mystics. All of it led me to nothing but frustration, failure, and emptiness.

Without God, I had no real hope. I could not see a future or a purpose for my life. But when I picked up my first Bible and had a pastor with the gift of teaching explain it to me, I fell in love—with the Bible and with God. I wanted to know all I could about His Word. I wanted to read as much as possible. And quickly, it became my true source of knowledge about God.

Subconsciously, while growing in knowledge of the Bible and God, I was also growing in faith. The book of Romans explains this phenomenon, "Faith comes from hearing the message, and the message is heard through the word of Christ" (10:17). I find this to be true even now that I'm considered a "longtime Christian." The more I read the Bible or listen to it being taught, the more my faith grows.

If you want to have strong faith, read your Bible every day. The Bible is not just any book. In fact, the apostle Paul wrote to his protégé, Timothy, "All scripture is God-breathed and is useful for teaching, rebuking, correcting, and training in righteousness" (2 Timothy 3:16). So memorize and meditate upon the Scriptures—they provide instruction for how to live your life. Examine everything through the filter of God's pure Word. And follow the examples of the many godly characters chronicled in the Bible. Let's take a look at, and learn from, some of the people in Scripture who lived lives of faith.

ABRAHAM, THE FATHER OF FAITH

For thousands of years, Christians everywhere have looked to Abraham as a model of faith. Why? Against all odds, God used Abraham—an elderly man with no land, no children, and a barren wife—to begin a new race of people, the Jewish people. His incredible story is told in Genesis, where we read: "The LORD had said to Abram, 'Leave your country, your people and your father's household and go to the land I will show you. I will make you into a great nation and I will bless you; I will make your name great, and you will be a blessing. I will bless those who bless you, and whoever curses you I will curse; and all peoples on earth will be blessed through you" (12:1–3).

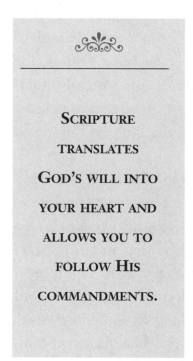

SCRIPTURE TRANSLATES GOD'S WILL INTO YOUR HEART AND ALLOWS YOU TO FOLLOW HIS COMMANDMENTS.

We don't know much about the early years of Abraham—then called "Abram"—and his relationship with God. However, it's obvious from this Scripture that God did not just give Abraham a promise, He also issued him a command.

It would be hard for anyone to leave his family and relatives. But imagine being told to leave your country and your roots as well. In Abraham's day, families lived in the same place for centuries. When they traveled, it was by foot or by camel—and more often than not, just to the next town. Unless you were a woman marrying into another family, you rarely left the home of your ancestors.

I know how stressful moving can be. Living in San Diego, I meet many people who are members of the military. It is not uncommon for these folks to pick up and move to another city or base every few years. What's more, the spouses of military personnel must stay home with the children while the soldier or sailor goes on a tour of duty for months at a time. This is all very difficult on marriages and families.

I'm willing to bet that Abraham was more than a little apprehensive about leaving his home of Haran. The Lord wasn't just promising him a blessed life—He also was telling him to go to the land of Canaan, a place he'd never seen. Personally, I don't see how he could have been motivated by God's promise alone. But Abraham responded in faith to the Lord's calling on his life; shortly after God spoke to him, he packed up his life and set out with his wife, his nephew, and all their possessions.

Abraham gave up everything for God, but for a long time he still faced family squabbles, infertility, and problems adjusting to foreign lands. It took time for God's promise of a son to come to fruition—about twenty-five years. Understandably, after years and years of waiting, Abraham began to doubt God's promise that he and Sarah would be granted any children, much less a whole nation of descendants. In fact, Abraham said despondently to God, "You have given me no children; so a servant in my household will be my heir" (Genesis 15:3). But God responded patiently and lovingly. "He took [Abram] outside and said, 'Look up at the heavens and count the stars—if indeed you can count them. Then he said to him, 'So shall your offspring be'" (15:5).

This Scripture illustrates Abraham's faith as it began to deepen. The story goes on to say that "Abram believed the LORD, and he credited it to him as righteousness" (Genesis 15:6). No longer skeptical, Abraham chose to trust in God and His Word. As a result, God was pleased by Abraham's depth of faith and called it "righteousness." Not long after, God sealed His promise to His servant, saying, "As for me, this is my covenant with you: You will be the father of many nations. No longer will you be called Abram; your name will be Abraham" (17:4–6).

In Old Testament times, names were much more significant

than they are today. Often they had literal meanings that were meant to convey specific qualities about or hopes for a person's life. According to *Strong's Exhaustive Concordance* the name Abram means "exalted father" while Abraham means "father of a multitude." God's act of renaming Abraham was more than just a nice gesture—it was a reaffirmation of His promise.

Today, Abraham's extended family is as numerous as God assured him it would be and is represented in the nations of the Middle East. The Arab nation comes from Ishmael, the son Abraham had with his wife's handmaiden, Hagar. And the Jewish nation comes from Abraham's son, Isaac, miraculously born to his ninety-year-old wife, Sarah. According to hundreds of stories in the Old Testament, Isaac's descendants were protected and blessed by God; the Jews became His chosen, favored people.

Oswald Chambers reflected on Abraham's life in his classic devotional *My Utmost for His Highest*: "Living a life of faith means never knowing where you are being led. But it does mean loving and knowing the One who is leading. It is literally a life of faith, not of understanding and reason—a life of knowing Him who calls us to go."

The book of Hebrews in the New Testament defines faith this way: "Now faith is the substance of things hoped for, the evidence of things not seen" (Hebrews 11:1 NKJV). I love this translation of Hebrews because it uses the word *substance*. God wants our hope to have meaning and definition to it. Just like Abraham, we all hope for things. But we often give up on them simply because we lack the vision for what God can do. The truth is, God can do anything! In fact, it appears that He even says somewhat facetiously to Abraham at one point, "Is anything too hard for the LORD?" (Genesis 18:14).

I take great comfort in Abraham's story. It reminds me that God has a roadmap for our lives, whether we believe it or not. It reminds me that He can do anything with us, no matter who we are or what the circumstances. Like all of us, Abraham had times of doubt—at one point, he even laughed at God's suggestion that he would become a father (Genesis 17:17). But ultimately he believed that God would do what He had promised.

GIDEON: AN UNLIKELY LEADER

Abraham's story is just one of countless tales of faith in the Bible. Another features an interesting character who faced seemingly insurmountable challenges and learned to trust God. His name was Gideon. The Old Testament book of Judges describes how God also commissioned Gideon, a nervous and doubtful young man, to do what seemed impossible—to rescue the Israelites from the oppressive Midianites.

For years, the Midianites had been swarming the Israelites' land like locusts, stealing their livestock, ruining their crops, and wreaking havoc. In order to feed their families, the Israelites were forced to harvest their crops in secret. At the time of the commissioning, God found Gideon in his father's winepress, where he was threshing wheat to keep it hidden from the Midianites. We pick up the story:

> The LORD turned to [Gideon] and said, "Go in the strength you have and save Israel out of Midian's hand. ..."
> "LORD," [he] asked, "how can I save Israel? My clan is the weakest in Manasseh, and I am the least in my family."

The LORD answered, "I will be with you, and you will strike down all the Midianites together" (Judges 6:14–16).

This was quite a promise. The Midianites had tortured Gideon's people for seven long years and commanded an enormous army. They appeared unbeatable—so formidable, in fact, that despite God's assurance of success, Gideon wondered whether victory was truly possible.

The night before the battle, he panicked. *What if it wasn't really God speaking to me?* he wondered. *What if I've been hearing things?* Fearful, he asked God for a sign. The Lord tried to reassure Gideon and gave him what he asked for. What did Gideon do? Like many of us probably would, he promptly asked for two more signs (see Judges 6:17–40). Again God responded, but Gideon continued to worry. Then on the morning of the battle, as the men were preparing to attack, God heightened the stakes: "The LORD said to Gideon, 'You have too many men for me to deliver Midian into their hands. In order that Israel may not boast against me that her own strength has saved her, announce now to the people, 'Anyone who trembles with fear may turn back and leave Mount Gilead'" (Judges 7:2–3).

Gideon was petrified, but with the small measure of faith God gave him, he did what the Lord asked. Twenty-two thousand men deserted, leaving Gideon with just ten thousand men—a fraction of the warriors in the Midianite army. But God told Gideon that he still had too many men and had Gideon order the remainder of them to go down to the river and drink. The men who kneeled down and drank directly from the river would be told to leave, and the ones who lapped the water out of their cupped hands would be allowed to stay and fight.

The men went down to the river, and of the ten thousand, only three hundred lapped the water from their hands. For someone who had just asked God three separate times for signs that he would be victorious, Gideon must have been horrified to be left with this pitiful remnant. But God was giving both Gideon and the Israelites a lesson in faith: As Gideon would soon learn, the battle was not his but God's.

That night, the Lord sent Gideon into the enemy's camp. While he was hiding behind some bushes, Gideon overheard two guards discussing a strange dream one of them had in which a loaf of bread fell from heaven and squashed the Midianite tent. In those days, many people had prophetic dreams, and the guard was spooked. His friend analyzed the dream, saying fearfully, "This can be nothing other than the sword of Gideon son of Joash, the Israelite. God has given the Midianites and the whole camp into his hands" (Judges 7:14).

> WHEN WE RELY ON GOD AND TRUST HIM, WE CAN CONQUER ANY PROBLEM OR SITUATION.

The guard's dire prediction spread through the Midianites' camp like wildfire, and the soldiers began to panic. Building on their fears, God gave Gideon a battle plan. Later that night, Gideon and his men were to surround the camp, each holding a torch, a clay pot, and a trumpet. Then Gideon was to give the Israelites a signal, and the three hundred men would blow their trumpets, break their clay pots, and shout, "The sword of the Lord and of Gideon!"

It sounds ridiculous, but the plan worked. The Israelites'

noise pierced the Midianites' sleeping camp and sent them into a frenzy. These mighty soldiers thought Gideon was commanding a fleet of chariots and that a huge, fierce army was upon them. Confused and stumbling around in the dark, they began swinging swords at their own comrades. Many more fled the scene, crying out as they ran. That day the Israelites subdued the Midianites, and Gideon led his countrymen to forty years of peace.

Elisabeth Elliot once wrote, "The eye of faith looks through and past that which the human eye focuses on." Gideon initially acted like a coward, but as Elliot describes, he was willing to look past the facts and focus on the supernatural—to enter into battle with nothing more than God's Word to help him fight. Just like Abraham—and all of us—he worried, he doubted, but he held on to God's promise. I love this story because it illustrates so vividly what God can do with a little bit of faith. It also reminds me that the Lord's ways are not our ways. Often he will design a strategy that does not seem to add up, but in the end, it not only proves to work, but it gives Him the glory as well.

We're not likely to face a battle scene like the one Gideon faced, but we do encounter battles each day that require us to exercise our faith. Many of these battles appear impossible to win. As we learn about God's faithfulness, though, we begin to understand that He will not let us falter. When we rely on God and trust Him, we, like Gideon, can conquer any problem or situation.

THE WAY TO VICTORY

The stories of Abraham and Gideon are powerful because they remind us we have a Creator who loves us and has our best interests at heart. Reading their incredible stories increases our faith immeasurably, building us up in several ways. Scripture reveals the blessings that God provides for His children, which gives us hope. The Bible also serves as our battle plan, giving us spiritual might.

Life is full of pitfalls, both physical and spiritual. Near our house in San Diego are canyons filled with brush, trees, flowers, squirrels, hawks, coyotes, and rattlesnakes. I love climbing down these sandstone cliffs and winding through the beautiful scenery. I've encountered lots of small critters and medium-sized animals while walking these trails, but one creature I don't want to meet is a rattlesnake. So I stay on the path, avoid overgrown parts of the trail, and whistle loudly. Our dog, however, is fearless. She wanders in the undergrowth and puts her long snout into holes and in between rocks. If she understood the danger posed by a rattler, she would be more cautious.

As my canyon walks illustrate, our physical environment can pose many threats. But the Bible also tells us the world poses spiritual threats. A spiritual war is waged every day of the week over the eternal souls of men, women, and children of every race, color, and creed. This battle is between the forces of good and evil, between God, who leads the forces of light, and the Devil, who rules as the prince of darkness.

Since the Bible says that we are to be active and aggressive participants in this battle, we need to be alert at all times. No other book in history is as clear as the Bible on the subject of spiritual warfare and the role of Christians in this battle. The apostle Paul wrote about this warfare to the early church in the city of Ephesus, telling the Ephesians to be vigilant. In his letter, which later became a book in the New Testament, he wrote:

Be strong in the Lord and in his mighty power. Put on the full armor of God so that you can take your stand against the devil's schemes. For our struggle is not against flesh and blood, but against the rulers, against the authorities, against the powers of this dark world and against the spiritual forces of evil in the heavenly realms. Therefore put on the full armor of God, so that when the day of evil comes, you may be able to stand your ground, and after you have done everything, to stand. Stand firm then, with the belt of truth buckled around your waist, with the breastplate of righteousness in place, and with your feet fitted with the readiness that comes from the gospel of peace. In addition to all this, take up the shield of faith, with which you can extinguish all the flaming arrows of the evil one. Take the helmet of salvation and the sword of the Spirit which is the word of God. And pray in the Spirit, on all occasions with all kinds of prayers and requests. With this in mind, be alert and always keep on praying for all the saints (6:10–18).

AS A PERSON OF FAITH, YOU HAVE PROTECTION IN THE FORM OF SPIRITUAL ARMOR.

Don't let spiritual warfare become a scary proposition for you. As a person of faith, you have protection in the form of spiritual armor! Sadly, after ministering so many years, I have found that most people don't realize this and fail to draw upon God's power. They get caught up in the busyness of the world and go through life without a bit of armor on them.

Abraham and Gideon endured many crises before God's promises came to fruition. What would have happened if Abraham had gone through his journey without an active faith? Or if Gideon had tried to go it alone, fighting the Midianites without the weapons of faith the Lord provided? God has given us tools to defend ourselves and to go on the offensive in our communities for the good of the Gospel. The book of Ephesians goes on to say that you, as a Christian, have a spiritual helmet, breastplate, sword, and shield. Do you use them? The apostle Paul states that the purpose of this spiritual armor—this God-given faith—is so that you may be able to stand against the wiles of the Devil.

This idea of spiritual warfare may be new to you. But whether you are hearing about spiritual warfare for the first or the fiftieth time, take some time to think and pray about this faith-building concept. When you do, God's Holy Spirit will reveal things to you that only He can teach.

ACCESS HIS POWER BY TAPPING INTO HIS WORD

As we've learned through the stories of Abraham and Gideon and from the words of the apostle Paul, it is God who provides us with faith—a faith that is active and powerful. This faith brings us closer to God, helps us achieve impossible tasks, enables us to overcome the snares of the Devil, and gives us the power to live in ways that are pleasing to God.

Like our relationships with our loved ones, our relationship with God should never be stagnant; we must always strive to continue growing in faith. The Bible is a great source of growth. Live a life of faith based on His Word and you cannot go wrong.

I'd like to challenge you to take some time in the next few days to find a nice quiet spot—somewhere the phone won't ring, the dog won't bark, and the television is not blaring. Memorize some verses that are especially meaningful to you, and take the time to think about how important the Bible is in your life.

Ask yourself, *What are the obstacles confronting me today?* Do you, like Abraham and Gideon, need assurance that God has a purpose for you? Are you facing change or impossible circumstances? No matter what you may be dealing with, the Bible can give you guidance and assistance. Another one of my favorite verses speaks directly to this: "Your word is a lamp to my feet and a light for my path" (Psalm 119:105).

If you want to live a life of incredible faith, read the Bible, learn the Scriptures, and apply them to your daily life. Let the inspired Word of God correct you and reprove you. Don't shy away from God's truth; let it have free reign to instruct you in righteous living. Your faith will grow the more you read and learn.

CHAPTER EIGHT

ADVERSITY IS AN ALLY

THE BIBLE SHOWS US HOW TO HANDLE HARDSHIPS AND HEARTACHES

We are always on the forge or on the anvil.
Through trials, God is shaping us for higher things.
HENRY WARD BEECHER

The ancient city of Antioch was a thriving seaport on the Mediterranean, just north of Lebanon. Ideally situated on the trade routes along the Red Sea and the Persian Gulf, Antioch was a melting pot for a rich mixture of people. It bustled with Syrians, Romans, Greeks, and Arabs and was known as much for its culture as for its commerce.

In the late 1930s, archeologists from Princeton University conducted excavations at the site of the ancient city. This project revealed beautiful mosaic floors, coins, and other important inscriptions and artifacts. But Antioch was more than just a vital cultural hub—it became an important center of growth for the early Christian church. It was the place where the apostle Paul began all three of his missionary journeys. It was the place where, according to many scholars, the gospels of Luke and Matthew were written. Most significantly, it was the place where followers of Jesus were first called "Christians" (see Acts 11:26).

It is inspiring to me that such an important commercial and communication center would be the first to give Christians their name. The Holy Spirit must have made a profound impact on that worldly populace for them to take such notice of the followers of Jesus! But what else do you suppose would cause such an upwardly mobile society to recognize a small sect of people who followed the teachings of a former carpenter?

I think we could safely say that ancient Christians must have lived in such a way that made their neighbors take notice. The manner in which Christians responded to daily problems and painful situations probably deeply affected the secular community in which they lived. How can followers of Jesus in the twenty-first century live so that others may take notice? I believe we should start by looking in the Bible, which provides every tool we need to deal with the challenges inherent in day-to-day living. Like our forebears in the faith, we can be a testimony to those around us by demonstrating grace in the midst of problems and peril.

STILL RELEVANT AFTER ALL THESE YEARS

I vividly remember listening to Pastor Chuck teach a Bible study from the Old Testament book of Isaiah. During the study, he told the story of Sir Edmund Allenby, a famous commander of British forces during World War I. It was nearing Christmas time, and Allenby was trying to get his troops into the old city of Jerusalem to remove the enemy stronghold there before the holidays began. It was a monumental task, so the general first had an army plane fly over the city for reconnaissance. Ever cautious, he wanted to pinpoint where his enemy was hiding so he could identify which area would muster the most resistance.

> THOSE WHO TRY TO GO IT ALONE OFTEN FEEL DEFEATED BY LIFE'S DIFFICULTIES.

Flying over the city with a single-engine airplane, the pilot flew low and slow. Well, the British got more than they expected from that mission! Apparently, their enemies thought they were going to be bombed from the air and immediately retreated from the city for safety. General Allenby marched in without causing any major damage to the old city of Jerusalem. A single plane had ended the standoff—and without a single shot fired.

As Pastor Chuck told the story, he related it to a verse in the book of Isaiah that says, "Like birds hovering overhead, the LORD Almighty will shield Jerusalem; he will shield it and deliver it, he will 'pass over' it and will rescue it" (31:5). God promised thousands of years ago that He would protect that ancient city—and He did not disappoint.

Hearing that verse as a young student of the Bible, I realized suddenly that Scripture could be as relevant for Christians today as it was thousands of years ago. God speaks through His

Word not only to tell us about who He is and what He promises, but also to remind us that the Bible can help us learn to deal with our present circumstances, no matter how daunting they may be. Like the Israelites four thousand years ago, we, too, can learn to trust in and lean on God.

THE BIBLE IS OUR SOURCE OF STRENGTH

Our church congregation in San Diego recently marked its thirty-year anniversary with a celebration and service at Mission Bay Park in San Diego. This large bay, with over two thousand acres under water, is a great place to water ski, Jet Ski, sail, and kayak. Joggers love running around the perimeter because of Mission Bay Park and its beautiful scenery. On that celebration Sunday, several thousand Christians sat on the grass facing the bay and worshiped God, giving thanks for three decades of fellowship. We had music, free barbecue, and plenty of rides and games for children. We also baptized hundreds of people, some who had just made decisions for Christ that morning.

After four hours in the sun, it was time to head home. As I walked through the parking lot, a group of teenage girls driving with their adult chaperone rolled down the windows and stopped me to say hello. All four of the girls had been baptized that morning. With wet hair and towels in their hands, and with beaming smiles, these girls told me that today had been "their day." I beamed back at them, knowing I had played a small part in a very large spiritual drama. Each of those girls had experienced and enjoyed what was probably the most significant chapter of her life story. I'll tell you why.

Baptism is always an exciting experience, because it represents a Christian's new life as a follower of Jesus Christ. For these girls, however, the baptism service was particularly poignant: They had recently been homeless. Now, fresh off the streets, they were being discipled by women in the church and had recently been placed in Christian homes. The Bible talks about accepting God's love and salvation as the beginning of a "new life" in a spiritual sense, but sometimes it happens in a practical sense as well. These girls were experiencing new life on many levels.

Standing in the parking lot, talking to these sweet, vivacious young women, I became overwhelmed with emotion. I got choked up. Their lives were an incredible testament to God's power. As I leaned on the rear car door, I spoke to them through the open window.

"Girls, you have had hard lives up until now," I said.

They nodded in agreement.

"But God has blessed you and forgiven your sins," I continued. "You have great futures ahead. You have the opportunity to become anything you put your minds to! Now forget the past and live for Jesus."

Looking at their glowing faces, I added, "It's not going to be easy. You're going to need to keep yourselves pure from sex and drugs and alcohol. And you need to love others like you are being loved now."

To an outsider, my instructions to them may have sounded unrealistic. How could these formerly homeless girls, who for years had been exposed to violence, prostitution, drugs, and despair, suddenly turn their lives around and follow God? Well, they could—and they did—because their strength came from the Lord. Over months of Bible study and fellowship, these girls developed an inner strength they had never before experienced. As they continued to read about Him, they were filled with the Holy Spirit and learned to rely on God for their needs.

King David described this kind of closeness with God when he said, "You are my portion, O LORD; I have promised to obey your words. I have sought your face with all of my heart; be gracious to me according to your promise. I have considered my ways and have turned my steps to your statutes. I will hasten and not delay to obey your commands" (Psalm 119:57–60).

If you and I hold on to God's Word and trust in Him, He will become our strength. Those who try to go it alone often feel defeated by life's difficulties—by the stress of challenging relationships or painful memories from the past. But the Bible reminds us repeatedly that we don't have to rely on ourselves. Our strength is in God. And He has given us His Word to live by—the perfect source of comfort and consolation.

THE BIBLE HELPS US LEARN FROM OTHERS

As a pastor of a large congregation, I've seen my fellow Christians confront every hardship imaginable. Whether it's infidelity, job loss, alcoholism, failing grades, or serious illness, difficulty can do one of two things: It can build righteous character or it can foster bitterness. You and I get the honor of choosing which path we are going take.

One of the reasons I love the Bible is that it gives me the power to prevail in negative circumstances, while telling the stories of those who have gone before me and chosen the narrow path, learning to find their hope in God. The Old Testament, for instance, is chock-full of anguished prayers from King David. For years his predecessor, King Saul, chased him all over the country in an effort to kill him and prevent him from taking the throne. Because of that, David was forced to leave his home and live like a refugee. In the process, he lost the companionship of his best friend, Jonathan, whom I mentioned in chapter 5. But David didn't let the crises in his life drive him away from God; his suffering brought him closer to the Lord.

To cope with his problems, David penned hundreds of prayers and songs to God, opening his heart with honesty and candor. David praised God, questioned God, and pleaded with God. For example, in just one of his countless prayers recorded in the Psalms, the young king wrote, "I cry aloud to the LORD; I lift up my voice to the LORD for mercy. I pour out my complaint before him; before him I tell my trouble. When my spirit grows faint within me, it is you who know my way" (Psalm 142:1–3).

GOD HAS GIVEN US HIS WORD TO LIVE BY—THE PERFECT SOURCE OF COMFORT AND CONSOLATION.

Like David, the apostle Paul also faced harrowing circumstances. He chronicled his plight in a letter to the church at Corinth:

Five times I received from the Jews the forty lashes minus one. Three times I was beaten with rods, once I was stoned, three times I was shipwrecked, I spent a night and a day in the open sea, I have been constantly on the move. I have been in danger from ... my own countrymen, in danger from Gentiles; in danger in the city, in danger in the country, in danger at sea; and in danger from false brothers.

*I have labored and toiled and have gone without
sleep; I have known hunger and thirst and have often
gone without food; I have been cold and naked. Besides
everything else, I face daily the pressure of my concern
for all the churches. Who is weak, and I do not feel
weak? Who is led into sin, and I do not inwardly burn?*
(2 Corinthians 11:24–29)

Talk about a rough go of it! What a tremendous list of sufferings Paul endured—all for the sake of the Gospel. That
puts into perspective the trials we face in our own lives,
doesn't it? But like David, Paul also turned to God in order
to make it through those dark hours. As a result, God not
only comforted him, but also gave him strength. Paul
described this turning point later: "[The Lord] said to me,
'My grace is sufficient for you, for my power is made perfect
in weakness.' Therefore I will boast all the more gladly about
my weaknesses, so that Christ's power may rest on me. That
is why, for Christ's sake, I delight in weaknesses, in insults,
in hardships, in persecutions, in difficulties. For when I am
weak, then I am strong" (2 Corinthians 12:9–10).

Here's the clincher: Although Paul experienced more suffering than most of us will ever face, he did not wallow in his
pain. He ultimately used his affliction and adversity to encourage others, penning numerous letters full of hope and exhortation to the early church. Listen to what Paul told the church in
Ephesus:

*I ask you, therefore, not to be discouraged because of
my sufferings for you, which are your glory. For this
reason I kneel before the Father, from whom his whole*

family in heaven and on earth derives its name. I pray
~~that out of his glorious riches he may strengthen you~~
with power through his Spirit in your inner being, so
that Christ may dwell in your hearts through faith.
And I pray that you, being rooted and established in
love, may have power, together with all the saints, to
grasp how wide and long and high and deep is the love
of Christ, and to know this love that surpasses knowl-
edge, that you may be filled to the measure of all the
fullness of God (Ephesians 3:13–19).

As you mature in your faith, you, too, will find opportunities to help others because you have "been there, done that." I don't mean that in a flippant way—it's the truth. When you have experienced God's strength in the midst of weakness, you become the perfect candidate to help those around you. You have more to give. You can encourage better, sympathize better, love better, and even pray better.

We cannot give what we do not have. If we want to love God and others deeply, if we want to help people in their faith, we too must have experienced pain—we also must have learned to find our strength in God.

THE BIBLE TELLS US HOW TO COPE WITH CRISES

One of the things I like most about being a pastor is helping our congregation work through challenges. That's right—I actually enjoy helping others work through their problems. Every week, I meet dozens of nice people from literally every walk of life. And whether I am conducting a wedding for a couple or counseling someone who is facing considerable loss, I get a sense of fulfillment from helping the people God brings into my life. As a result of the years I've spent as a minister, I've come up with five principles—with corresponding Scripture verses—for handling life's setbacks.

These Scriptures are what I like to call "life verses"—verses that leap off the page when you're reading the Bible. These types of verses become like old friends, and they show up just when you need them. If you are struggling with something in your life and seeking direction or encouragement from the Bible, I think you'll be amazed at what God shows you. These verses have stayed in my heart for years and have helped me deal with tough times in my own life. I hope these principles will help you, too.

Principle #1: Forget the Past—Reach for the Future

"Brothers, I do not consider myself yet to have taken hold of it. But one thing I do: Forgetting what is behind and straining toward what is ahead, I press on toward the goal to win the prize for which God has called me heavenward in Christ Jesus" (Philippians 3:13–14).

Are you holding on to past trauma or mistakes? There's certainly value in evaluating your actions and learning from the past, and it's equally important that you give yourself time to heal from crisis. But don't let yourself wallow in it. In my work I often see people who have become paralyzed by their memories, seemingly unable or unwilling to look at the fresh hope God offers for their future. When this happens I have to tell them it's time to forgive themselves, forgive others, and with God's help move forward. I do not intend to short-circuit the healing process and I certainly don't want to give pat answers. But there really does come a time when we must decide to "forget what is behind" and believe by faith that God forgets it too.

Fortunately, the New Testament is full of encouragement for those who are having difficulty letting go of the past. Throughout Paul's second letter to the church at Corinth, he referred to the intense suffering he experienced for the sake of the Gospel. But Paul kept his eyes on God's promises and reminded himself and his audience that they must press on, saying, "For our light and momentary troubles are achieving for us an eternal glory that far outweighs them all" (2 Corinthians 4:17).

If you stand in one spot too long you will become stagnant. So I encourage you to do whatever is necessary to work through your hardships and heartaches, and then press on for Jesus. Life is short, and we have "eternal glory" awaiting us.

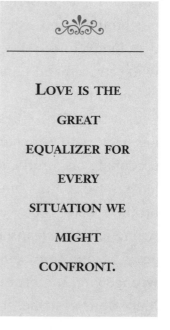

LOVE IS THE GREAT EQUALIZER FOR EVERY SITUATION WE MIGHT CONFRONT.

Principle #2: Practice Forgiveness

"Do not judge, and you will not be judged. Do not condemn, and you will not be condemned. Forgive, and you will be forgiven" (Luke 6:37).

Your sibling betrays a confidence. Your spouse has a long-term affair—with your "best friend." Your roommate steals your CD collection before moving out. A coworker spreads a damaging and false rumor about you. Sometimes our suffering is a direct result of the sins of others rather than simply due to unfortunate circumstances. When others cause us pain, it's easy to hang on to that feeling of being wronged and wallow in our bitterness.

Despite our suffering, however, the Bible commands us to forgive. As I said in chapter 5, forgiveness is one of the most popular topics in Scripture. Jesus repeatedly tells us to forgive our brothers and sisters. And throughout the Bible, He practices forgiveness, refusing to be angry and bitter at the people who betrayed and ultimately killed Him.

So if the Bible instructs us to forgive, why do we struggle with it so much? I believe it's because forgiveness ultimately has to do with our character, our pride. Our ego keeps us from pardoning our brothers and sisters. Once we are finally able to let go of our hurt and heed God's command to forgive our brothers and sisters, we will find freedom. Forgiveness is a strong spiritual cleanser. It gets down into those dark and dusty areas of our souls and scours the stain of sin, the scars of wrongdoing, the bruises of transgressions. Bible teacher John MacArthur describes it like this: "Forgiveness unleashes joy. It brings peace. It washes the slate clean. It sets all the highest values of love in motion. In a sense, forgiveness is Christianity at its highest level."[1]

Principle #3: Let Go of Your Fear

"For God has not given us a spirit of fear, but of power and of love and of a sound mind" (2 Timothy 1:7 NKJV).

No matter what circumstances you might face, you do not need to be fearful. The Lord is a God of love, and He will give you everything you need to handle life's challenges. He will give you power when you run out of strength, love when you feel despair, and peace when you feel anxious.

If there was anyone in the Bible who could have been worried about the challenges facing her it was Queen Esther. She was married to the Persian King Xerxes after he'd deposed his former wife and then conducted a nationwide search for virginal young beauties. Nice guy. Esther was selected by the king, but she had a potentially dangerous secret: She was a Jew. In the kingdom in which Esther lived, the Jewish people were a minority and had not assimilated well into the Persian way of life. Concerned about what might happen to her, Esther's uncle, Mordecai, forbade her to tell the king about her heritage.

Esther had not lived in the palace for long when King Xerxes's wicked aide Haman convinced him to kill all the Jews in the kingdom. Moving quickly, Mordecai encouraged Esther to use her position to protect the Jews. Esther was understandably reluctant to disclose the truth to Xerxes—just calling on the king without his invitation was against the law and could have resulted in her death. But Mordecai encouraged her to do it, telling her that God had placed her in the palace "for such a time as this."

Esther summoned her courage and trusted God to see her through the situation. She petitioned the king, asking him to spare the Jews, and God protected her and the Jewish people. And in the end it was Haman rather than Esther or Uncle Mordecai who hung from the gallows.

I find Esther's story extremely encouraging. It reminds me

that God ordains all our circumstances, and that He will provide the strength to help us deal with any situation. If you are facing tough times, ask God to give you courage. It may be that you, like Esther, were created "for such a time as this."

Principle #4: Seek Direction from God's Word

> *"The wisdom that is from above is first pure, then peaceable, gentle, and easy to be entreated, full of mercy and good fruits, without partiality, and without hypocrisy" (James 3:17 KJV).*

Have you ever wondered what God's will is for you today? Do you ever worry about what career path to take or whom you should marry or where you should live? If you are preoccupied about what direction your life is headed, then memorize the Scripture above. It lists what I like to call the seven signs of wisdom from heaven: purity, peacefulness, consideration, submissiveness, mercy, impartiality, and sincerity. If your career choice or potential spouse meets the above criteria, you can rest easy that God is directing you that way.

The Bible is the best tool for us to gauge whether we are on the right track. The late author Frederick C. Grant talked about the power of Scripture to lead us through every part of our lives:

> *We are frequently advised to read the Bible with our own personal needs in mind and to look for answers to our own private questions. That is good, but better still is the advice to study the Bible objectively ... without regard, first of all, to our own subjective needs.*

Let the great passages fix themselves in our memory. Let them stay there permanently, like bright beacons, launching their powerful shafts of light upon life's problems—our own and everyone's—as they illumine, now one, now another dark area of human life. Following such a method, we discover that the Bible does "speak to our condition" and meet our needs, not just occasionally or when some emergency arises, but continually.[2]

Take some time to read the Bible the way the author described above. Meditate on the verses that seem to jump off the page. You will be surprised by what God shows you.

Principle #5: Above All, Love

"Love the Lord your God with all your heart and with all your soul and with all your mind. ... Love your neighbor as yourself" (Matthew 22:37, 39).

WE CAN BE A TESTIMONY TO THOSE AROUND US BY DEMONSTRATING GRACE IN THE MIDST OF PROBLEMS AND PERIL.

Life is usually spent on the defensive. We duck fly balls, swerve to miss other cars, and avoid people we don't want to see. We build walls—both emotional and physical—to protect ourselves. We tend to live as if others are out to get us, and we do everything we can to avoid getting hurt. Here's a principle to keep things in perspective: Love is the great equalizer for every situation we might confront. No matter what the circumstances, whether we have been wronged or are simply reeling from the challenges of life, we are called to love both God and others.

One of the best stories of selfless love is in the Old Testament book of Ruth. It tells the story of Naomi, who was driven out of her hometown of Bethlehem by famine and forced to move with her husband to the strange land of Moab. The family stayed there for several years, and Naomi's sons married two Moabite women, Orpah and Ruth. Not long after, Naomi's husband and her two sons died, leaving the three women destitute and alone. Brokenhearted, Naomi made plans to return to Israel once the famine was over and bid her daughters-in-law good-bye.

Orpah embraced her mother-in-law and left. But Ruth clung to Naomi with a fierce love, telling her, "Don't urge me to leave you or turn back from you. Where you go I will go, and where you stay I will stay. Your people will be my people and your God my God" (Ruth 1:16). This was quite a sacrifice on Ruth's part. Not only did she leave her heritage and country, but she also chose to go with a widow who was so grief-stricken that her very countenance had changed. Sad and angry, the once-pleasant Naomi had begun telling her fellow Israelites to call her "Mara," which means "bitter."

Ruth was hurting perhaps as much as Naomi was, but she chose to focus on loving her mother-in-law. In the end, because of Ruth's selfless love, God blessed them both. Ruth married a kind man, Boaz, who took care of both women. Ruth gave birth to a son named Obed, who grew up and had a son named Jesse. Jesse eventually had a son named David.

And the promise of the Messiah came through the family line of David, the king of Israel.

There are hundreds of similar stories in the Bible that describe how God's people persevered through difficulty. Those stories, along with the promises and assurances presented in God's Word, can give us all the encouragement we need to face life's inevitable trials.

IT'S ALL ABOUT ATTITUDE

As a longtime beachgoer and ocean lover, I was captivated by the story of Bethany Hamilton, who was once ranked as the best amateur teen surfer in Hawaii. She survived a harrowing ordeal when a tiger shark attacked her while she was surfing. And although she escaped with her life, she lost an arm almost at the shoulder.

Through the period of recovery and beyond, she demonstrated an amazing attitude. Soon after the attack, she began to raise money to restore a man's eyesight. While visiting New York City, she gave her ski coat to a homeless girl. When asked about the gift, she said she had more than she needed in life.

Commenting on her resilience, an article in *USA Today* said, "As always, Hamilton remains undaunted. She has told her father that if having only one arm proved detrimental to reaching the top in competitive surfing, then she'd see about playing soccer."[3]

Her pastor, Steve Thompson, said, "She's looking forward to the future. She's asking herself, 'How can I show the world I still have a life, that I enjoy my life, and that my life is filled with joy?' She has an underlying trust that God is taking care of her."

That young lady's joyful attitude is a great encouragement and inspiration to me. I want to have that same positive, optimistic outlook when I encounter problems (which will probably be nothing like the problems Bethany has dealt with).

There's no doubt about it—we're all living in a world of hurt, a world in which we must deal with troubles and tragedies. Life is difficult for every person on planet earth, Christian or not. If you are a Christian, however, the difference is how you handle those crises. Do you turn to quick fixes? Easy escapes? Or do you first go to God? Do you seek to grow through painful experiences, or do you allow bitterness to take root?

If you are facing sorrow, loss, or challenge, take heart and turn to the Bible. When you do, God will be there for you, showing you just the right verse or story at just the right time, giving you fresh strength and courage to face each new day.

Chapter Nine

Getting Better All the Time

Becoming a Student of the Bible Enables You
to Continually Grow and Develop

*God loves us the way we are, but He loves us
too much to have us stay that way.*
Leighton Ford

Franklin Graham invited me to join him on a trip to Bosnia and Croatia during the dead of winter in 1995. At that time, the entire region was wracked with conflict, and many people had died in the battle between those two countries.

The purpose of our trip was to participate in a program with Samaritan's Purse, the relief ministry that Franklin leads. Specifically, we joined with other people as part of "Operation Christmas Child," an outreach that distributes shoeboxes filled with gifts to needy children. Though most of the areas in which we gave out shoeboxes were Muslim communities, the love of God bridged any gap of religious differences.

Everywhere we went, we witnessed the ravages of war. In one destitute and badly damaged town we traveled to, schoolchildren waited hours for our little caravan of cars and trucks to arrive with Christmas gifts. At the school where we were to distribute the shoeboxes, several of the classrooms had large holes in the walls caused by light artillery rounds and rocket-propelled grenades. To make matters worse, there was no heat or electricity in the classrooms. Since it was wintertime, Jack Frost nipped at our noses with a vengeance.

> GOD IS NOT FINISHED WITH THIS OLD WORLD YET—AND HE WON'T STOP LOVING AND CARING AND REACHING PEOPLE UNTIL HE'S READY.

The faces of the children appeared old for their ages. They stood in groups holding hands and hugging each other. They looked upon us Americans with apprehension more than with suspicion. After living in fear and danger for so long, these kids must have wondered what exactly these foreigners were doing there.

Country singer Ricky Skaggs and his wife, Sharon, who are longtime supporters of Samaritan's Purse, eased the tension and brought a sense of warmth to the cold, dank classrooms as they sang songs and played guitars. One of the schoolteachers began dancing to the music, and before long the entire class lined up behind her and formed a moving chain. Other teachers placed their cold hands on the backs of others in front of them and began to sing and move like a swaying caterpillar through the hallway and into the next classroom. The students circled the room with all the energy and enthusiasm of opening night at the Grand Ole Opry. Nashville had landed in Bosnia.

I can remember to this day the bitter chill of the frigid air. We were all dressed with thermal insulation, warm and comfortable boots, layers of clothing, with scarves wrapped tightly around our necks. We kept our heavy jackets on while we laughed and sang children's songs. Eventually, the spirit of celebration and gift-giving seemed to dispel some of the bone-chilling air.

In my many years of global travel, I have marveled at the conditions people can find themselves living in. This group of people didn't have running water, let alone heat or electricity. But they did have joy, love, and appreciative hearts.

In a town where the only bridge that crossed the river between it and the outside world had been blown up, these resilient people filled in the area of destruction with dirt, rocks, and anything of substance so we could cross the river. We were told that they had just finished filling in the chasm only hours before we arrived. They did not have a clue who we were—just that we were Americans coming to bless the children of Bosnia and Croatia.

Later, crossing back over that somewhat forbidding makeshift bridge, which was built with the painstaking help of most of the townspeople, I realized that the love of Jesus had just done a miracle before my eyes. For centuries, Catholics and Protestants have had their spats. Christians and non-Christians have battled, neighbor pitted against neighbor all in the name of "religion." But in the name of Jesus, I had witnessed passionate Christians delivering gifts of love to the battered and weary Muslim community. I was greatly impressed with Samaritan's Purse and Operation Christmas Child, because this program truly brings the love of Jesus where it has never penetrated before.

As our group departed that day—feeling joyful and grateful to be ambassadors of God's love—I couldn't help but think of something the apostle Paul wrote centuries ago:

> *"All over the world this gospel is bearing fruit and growing, just as it has been doing among you since the day you heard it and understood God's grace in all its truth" (Colossians 1:6).*

The Gospel of Jesus, the truth of His love and redemption, does indeed continue to grow and bear fruit. That's because God is not finished with this old world yet—and He won't stop loving and caring and reaching people until He's ready. There's another reason God's love continues to spread throughout the world: The Holy Spirit continues to work in the lives of individual Christians to cause growth, maturity, and a deeper understanding of His ways. As followers of Christ learn to think and act the way Jesus did, they become more and more effective at spreading the good news of God's love.

CHRISTIANS, TRUE AND FALSE

What is it that makes the difference between a "true, passionate Christian" and a "Christian church attendee"? What allows the vision of Franklin Graham and others like him to tackle the unthinkable, the seemingly impossible?

Unfortunately, the world is full of people who call themselves Christians but have no connection with heaven whatsoever. They describe themselves as a "Christian" because they grew up in a "Christian home" or because they live in a "Christian country." What the world needs today more than ever are real live representatives for Jesus Christ. The world needs more ambassadors for Jesus who will spread the good news of His kingdom to everyone they come into contact with.

Do you know where the word *Christian* originated? The Bible tells us in Acts 11:26: "The disciples were called Christians first at Antioch," which is the ancient city we discussed in the previous chapter. The word *Christian* comes from the Greek term meaning "followers of Christ." Some have translated the word to mean "Christlike" or "little Christs." I like that word picture, don't you? The Christian, then, is a reflection of Jesus. We are to live, walk, and talk like "little Christs" and to have Christlike actions and attitudes.

The hard part for me is that I don't always represent Jesus as I should. I don't know about you, but for me it is often difficult to behave like a Christian. Before my dear mother-in-law, Dottie, went to heaven, she used to say, "Getting old is not for sissies!" The same could be said for the Christian life: It isn't for sissies! Being a Christian is contrary to everything within our human nature, and it is absolutely counter to everything this world has to offer and all that it stands for.

Because the Christian life demands so much of us—because growth is usually a process of "two steps forward, one step back"—many people give up. They either abandon the faith altogether or remain stuck in place. The writer of Hebrews says that stagnant believers are like babies who can handle only milk. Growing believers, however, can chew on "meatier" truths:

> *Though by this time you ought to be teachers, you need someone to teach you the elementary truths of God's word all over again. You need milk, not solid food! Anyone who lives on milk, being still an infant, is not acquainted with the teaching about righteousness. But solid food is for the mature, who by constant use have trained themselves to distinguish good from evil (Hebrews 5:12–14).*

Every person new to the Christian faith starts out as an infant. Everything is fresh, mysterious, and sometimes perplexing. We have to take baby steps as we learn and develop. Some people, however, never get beyond that newborn stage. For any number of reasons—lack of encouragement, lack of motivation, lack of discipline—they fail to grow up in the faith.

One of the keys to Christian growth is to surround ourselves with other believers. We all need like-minded people who love the Bible, read together, pray together, and study together. One of the things that kept me going as a baby Christian was a peer group that loved Jesus and loved studying the Bible as I did. To sit in church with people my age made it more acceptable. I was twenty-six when I dedicated my life to God, and I felt that I was in good company because so many young people were coming to the Lord at the same time. We would underline Scriptures together and read to one another a new verse that seemed to jump out of the Bible at us. We discussed passages, debated ideas, and urged each other on as our faith deepened.

Looking back over many years, I know there were thousands of us who came to God during the Jesus Movement of the sixties. Those who were committed to God's Word are the ones still walking with Him. But those who just had "an experience" and did not become a disciple through His Scriptures fell by the wayside.

DON'T STOP GROWING

In the movie *Walking Across Egypt,* an elderly widow named Mattie is inspired by her pastor's sermon to care for "the least of these"—the less fortunate and downtrodden. So she decides to help a troubled sixteen-year-old boy, Wesley, whose parents abandoned him as a baby and who is serving time in a correctional center for stealing a car.

> **WHAT THE WORLD NEEDS TODAY MORE THAN EVER ARE REAL LIVE REPRESENTATIVES FOR JESUS CHRIST.**

After Mattie visits Wesley at the youth facility a couple of times, he breaks out and goes to her house. Thinking he is on authorized leave, she agrees to let him stay with her for a short time. He is a lovable but devious freeloader who wants to pilfer what he can from the kind old lady.

Eventually, Wesley is apprehended and returned to the center. But Mattie's compassion for the boy only grows—even though her adult children, Robert and Elaine, are alarmed and angered by her involvement with Wesley. They adamantly try to dissuade their mom from going further.

"He's an escaped convict," Elaine argues. "You could be charged with aiding and abetting a criminal."

"He's not a criminal, Elaine," Mattie snaps.

Robert disagrees. "He's a thief, Mama. He's a juvenile delinquent."

Mattie says, "Robert, nobody ever loved him."

"If they did," Robert retorts, "he probably stole their car."

Mattie begins to respond, "The Bible says—"

But she is interrupted by Elaine. "We know what the Bible says. The Bible is full of wonderful stories, Mama. It is a monument to humanity, but that's all it is. It's just a storybook."

Mattie is undeterred. "The good Lord says that we must help the least of these thy brethren. That boy is one of the least of these."

"I'll say!" Robert growls.

"You have already done plenty for him," Elaine says. "You have done more than most would. Doesn't the Bible say when to stop?"

Mattie emphatically replies: "No!"

That delightful scene underscores a theme woven throughout the Bible: Don't stop! Don't stop loving. Don't stop giving. Don't stop caring. As the apostle Paul said, "Let us not become weary in doing good, for at the proper time we will reap a harvest if we do not give up. Therefore, as we have opportunity, let us do good to all people" (Galatians 6:9–10). And later, John writes, "Let him who does right continue to do right; and let him who is holy continue to be holy" (Revelation 22:11).

What's more, we're not to stop learning, growing, and maturing. The apostle Peter points out several areas believers should continue to develop: faith, goodness, knowledge, self-control, perseverance, godliness, kindness, and love. Then he says, "For if you possess these qualities in increasing measure, they will keep you from being ineffective and unproductive. ... But if anyone does not have them, he is nearsighted and blind" (2 Peter 1:8–9).

Hear me loud and clear: The Bible is a book of momentum and forward progress. There are literally hundreds of references to words such as *continue, progress, mature, grow, increase,* and *carry on.* God wants you to keep getting better and better. He wants you to keep growing into the person He intends you to be. He wants you to fully use the gifts and talents you have been given.

God has put you here on earth for a reason. He has created you with a mission to fulfill, and He will continue working with you to accomplish it. As the psalmist said, "The LORD will fulfill his purpose for me; your love, O LORD endures forever" (138:8). And later, Paul added, "He who began a good work in you will carry it on to completion until the day of Christ Jesus" (Philippians 1:6).

Not long ago, I received the following e-mail from a dear lady in our church:

> *Falling in love with the Bible can come at times in your life when you least expect it. As a child, I grew up going to a Lutheran church with my mom and Catholic mass with my dad. The Bible wasn't real or tangible to me then. It didn't mean anything.*
>
> *Years later, I came to Horizon Church. I remember sitting in the auditorium, listening to the words preached and songs sung. And then I walked out. That was it.*
>
> *But then weeks later, I found myself lying on the*

top bunk of a cell at Las Colinas [Women's Prison] at one of the lowest times of my life. I heard a still, small voice say to me, "Ask for a Bible," and I did. I read it and devoured it, and it imprinted on my heart. It made sense for the first time ever. My cellmate was in jail for the murders of five people, and God revealed to my heart that I didn't belong there. I was expecting a five- to seven-year sentence, but when I went to court five days later, the judge said, "I am going to show mercy toward you." I was released with probation. Believe me, I left a changed person.

The very next week, I showed up at Horizon Church and heard the Bible taught—really taught— for the first time. Well, here I am fourteen years later, in fellowship, constantly pushed up on the road by my friends. I consult God every day, all day long, in my prayers. I love my Bible as much today as I did that day in that dark, icky cell. His Word is true. His Word is all I need.

GOD CREATED YOU WITH A MISSION TO FULFILL, AND HE WILL CONTINUE WORKING WITH YOU TO ACCOMPLISH IT.

Weeks ago, I was driving with my grandson, and I asked him, "What will you tell your kids and grandkids about me?" He said he would tell them how I took him on vacations, and I was the first one he saw when he was born (as I had delivered him).

*"What do you think is the one thing about me that
I want them all to know?" I asked.*

*He said, "That's so easy, Grandma—that you love
Jesus."*

He sure got that right!

Leann

This is the kind of life change that happens when someone
falls in love with the Bible. Whatever your background—
whether troubled or tame, stormy or stable—you can continue
growing with God's help. Becoming a devoted student of the
Bible will change everything about your life for the better.

IF YOU WANT TO GET STRONG, EAT YOUR FOOD

Just a couple of weeks ago, I was invited to speak on a Sunday
morning at a church in Northern California. I love the church
I help lead in San Diego, and being with them on Sunday is a
high priority and one of my greatest joys. So, it was with some
reluctance that I accepted the out-of-town speaking invitation.

On the designated Sunday, I delivered my sermon and
stood at the front of the sanctuary greeting people and shaking
hands. Before long, a man about my age came up and introduced himself.

"Hi, Mike," he said. "You may not remember me, but I used
to attend your church in San Diego." He gave me his name and
then added, "I went to your church for quite a while, but that
was about ten years ago."

Though it had been a decade since I'd seen him, I could
vaguely remember his face. During the discussion that ensued,
he made a passing remark that he was just now beginning to

read the Bible on a daily basis. That caught my "pastoral attention" because earlier he had mentioned that he'd been a Christian for twenty years.

Wow! I thought. *How could you go twenty years of your life claiming to be a Christian but never feasting on the Bread of Life?*

Please listen to my plea: Don't go a day without reading the Bible and praying. Don't let a week slip through your fingers without reading the Scriptures. God speaks through the Bible. And just like the manna from heaven that God gave to the children of Israel while they were in the wilderness for forty years, God will provide fresh spiritual food for you every day through the Scriptures.

Consistent reading and study of Scripture is a primary part of God's plan for our growth and development. Still, it can be a struggle and a challenge to grow in our understanding of God's truths. We are stretched and pulled and pushed as we grow in new ways. I agree with author Elisabeth Elliot, who said:

> *It appears that God has deliberately left us in a quandary about many things. Why did He not summarize all the rules in one book, and all the basic doctrines in another? He could have eliminated the loopholes, prevented all the schisms over morality and false teaching that have plagued His church for two thousand years. Think of the squabbling and perplexity we would have been spared. And think of the crop of dwarfs He would have reared! He did not spare us. He wants us to reach maturity. He has so arranged things that if we are to go on beyond the "milk diet," we shall be forced to think.*[1]

Growth does not come easily or quickly. It demands of us brainpower as well as willpower. When we study the Word of God and learn His truths, we must then seek to live out in our lives what has gone into our heads.

NEW EVERY MORNING

When you fall in love with the Bible, you will fall in love with God for several reasons. Three of those reasons are found in a passage written by King Solomon: "It is of the LORD's mercies that we are not consumed, because his compassions fail not. They are new every morning: great is thy faithfulness" (Lamentations 3:22–23 KJV).

God's character is full of compassion that never fails. It is as reliable as it is replenishing to our spirits. How wonderful to know that mercy is not a flippant word to God. If God were to withhold His compassion and mercy toward any one of us, we would be consumed in an instant.

King David understood very well the source of strength and security God is to us. As he wrote:

> **THE BIBLE IS A BOOK OF MOMENTUM AND FORWARD PROGRESS.**

O God, You are my God; early will I seek You; my soul thirsts for You; my flesh longs for You in a dry and thirsty land where there is no water. So I have looked for You in the sanctuary, to see Your power and Your glory. Because Your lovingkindness is better than life, my lips shall praise You (Psalm 63:1–3 NKJV).

Scholars tell us that David wrote this psalm while he was living in the wilderness. It was a hard time for the king, as his son Absalom was in rebellion and dividing his father's kingdom. It is gut-wrenching for any parent to battle with a child over any issue; far more so if you happen to be arguing about a kingdom that God has given you to rule. The kingdom was not to be turned over to Absalom, but this handsome young man let his pride get the best of him. Elsewhere, we are told that he died a tragic death (see 2 Samuel 18).

You can see the surrounding circumstances of David crying out in his prayer, "O God, You are my God; early will I seek You." David did not want to start a day in the wilderness without God by his side. It was a daily ritual for David to seek God early and begin his day with God leading him on paths of righteousness.

This is a great example for us to see the importance of reading the Bible every day. When we read a simple prayer like David's, the Holy Spirit can inspire us and encourage us. Without reading the Scriptures, we lose sight of what matters in life and what our existence on earth is really all about. David was a national hero, but also someone well acquainted with sorrow. David was, just like Jesus Christ, "despised and rejected by men, a Man of sorrows and acquainted with grief" (Isaiah 53:3 NKJV). We have all felt rejected and sorrowful at some point. The Bible reminds us that we are not alone, and that the great God of faithfulness understands our personal situations.

Bible reading and study have a cumulative affect, and the benefits increase as time goes on. I appreciate the perspective offered by Bible teacher Haddon Robinson:

We like to think that when we study the Bible, it's like getting a shot of spiritual adrenaline. We would like it to give us a spiritual high. But studying the Bible is much more like taking vitamins. You gulp down a couple of vitamins in the morning, but no wave of energy flows through your body. You take the vitamins because they build you up. They protect you against the diseases in the environment. In the long pull, they make you strong.[2]

That is so true. We are steadily and slowly strengthened as we learn from the Word of God how to walk by faith in Him. If you want to grow ever stronger and more satisfied, listen as God speaks to you through His book. If you want to enjoy ongoing growth and improvement, commit yourself to becoming a student of the Scriptures. Studying the Bible is an investment that pays huge dividends.

CHAPTER TEN

MINING FOR GOLD

IF YOU CONSISTENTLY DIG INTO THE BIBLE, YOU WILL DISCOVER UNIMAGINABLE RICHES

The Scriptures are shallow enough for a babe to come and drink without fear of drowning and deep enough for a theologian to swim in without ever touching the bottom.

ST. JEROME

In the movie *The Hurricane*, based on real-life events, Denzel Washington plays boxer Rubin "Hurricane" Carter, a man whose dreams of winning a prize title were destroyed when he was arrested and convicted for the 1966 murders of three people. Serving three natural life terms, Carter channels his frustration and despair by writing an autobiography from his cell.

Several years after the book is published, an alienated

173

young black man named Lezara is learning to read with three white mentors who have taken him into their Toronto home. One of his three friends takes him to a used book sale, where he picks up Carter's book.

"How do you know which book to pick?" Lezara asks.

His friend wisely answers, "Sometimes we don't pick the books we read. They pick us."

Lezara finds purpose and inspiration in Carter's story and begins writing letters to Hurricane. A mentoring relationship develops, and eventually Lezara's friends take up Carter's cause and vow to fight for his release from prison. Carter, at first skeptical of Lezara's white friends, is won over by their compassionate dedication. He later tells Lezara, "Hate put me in prison. Love is gonna bust me out."

His twenty-year fight for justice ends in triumphant freedom, and he celebrates the victory with his "little brother," the young man inspired by his book. Toward the end of the movie, while waiting for the judge's ruling, Hurricane asks young Lezara, "What was the first book you ever bought?"

"Yours," he answers.

"Do you think that was an accident?" Hurricane asks.

"No."

At that moment, young Lezara was no doubt thinking back to the words of his mentor: "Some books pick us."

> YOUR LIFE CAN BE CHANGED FOR THE BETTER IN EVERY WAY AS YOU LISTEN TO GOD SPEAK TO YOU THROUGH HIS BOOK.

The Bible is such a book. You can't read it without getting the sense that it picked you, that the Author had you in mind as He wrote. Your life can be turned upside-down and changed for the better in every way as you listen to God speak to you through His book.

Even though the Bible does "pick" some of us, many people choose not to pick (and pick up) the Bible. An interesting research project by George Barna shows how Americans look at the Bible. His report revealed that 71 percent of born-again Christians are "more than twice as likely as non-Christians to read the Word in a given week." (I am assuming the non-Christians are church attendees.) He goes on to say, "Similarly, those who attend evangelical churches are much more likely (72 percent) to open the Bible than either mainline Protestants (54 percent) or Catholics (26 percent)."[1]

Finally, one of the findings that jumped out at me was this: "Overall, 15 percent of the Christians read the Bible one day a week, 28 percent read it between two and six days a week, and 12 percent say they read it daily."[2]

I am always saddened to learn that many Christians don't avail themselves of the Bible every day, or at least several times a week. God wants to bless us, instruct us, guide us, and talk with us—and the way He does that most clearly and most powerfully is through the Scriptures.

THROUGH HIS WORD,
GOD MEETS US WHERE WE ARE

Children always provide a good balance for us older people. I love children—probably because I am the world's oldest living boy. In many ways, it is true that we have to grow up and be responsible. But in another way, we don't have to grow up if that means being serious, grumpy, and narrow-minded. All of us—whether two years old or a hundred and two—should retain a sense of wonder, awe, and surprise about life. I think this was what Jesus was getting at when He said, "Assuredly, I say to you, unless you are converted and become as little children, you will by no means enter the kingdom of heaven" (Matthew 18:3 NKJV). He wants us to delight in Him as a child delights in each new discovery.

From the time I was very young, I have always enjoyed automobiles. When I was a teenager, I had to fix my own cars because I didn't have money to pay a professional mechanic. In those days, you could actually fit your hand and a wrench between the fender and the exhaust manifold. Replacing a generator or removing the radiator was a rite of passage for teenage boys.

Like most of my peers, I liked fast cars the best. I never owned expensive cars, but I did have fast cars when I was in high school. I remember driving north on Sandy Boulevard on a warm, sunny morning in Portland, Oregon, when I was nineteen years old. (I'm sure I recall this incident so clearly because a warm, sunny day in Portland is so rare.) Coming out of a side street and headed in the opposite direction was a bright red 1963 Corvette Stingray convertible. That's a car that turns heads—and it did mine.

Besides the ideal weather, I remember that occasion for a number of reasons. First, it occurred next to a city landmark, the 7 UP bottling plant. Second, the driver was a gray-haired man. The juxtaposition struck me: It seemed strange that an older man was driving a hot rod. And third, it was 1963, so that was a brand-new body style for the Corvette.

I said to myself as I drove past him, *Hey, now that guy is cool.* I hope I'll be cool when I'm an old man. Honestly, that guy had probably just turned forty—but to a teenager, gray hair is gray hair. Today, I am well past forty with plenty of gray hair, and I hope that young people look at me and say, *Now that guy is cool.* At least I can take heart from the proverb that says, "The silver-haired head is a crown of glory, if it is found in the way of righteousness" (Proverbs 16:31 NKJV).

My point is this: I think back to when I was a kid and I think about myself as a "mature" man now, and I know the Bible is relevant all along the age continuum. You may not think that a gray-haired man who reads the Bible is cool—but you might just be wrong. We need to approach the Bible as *our* book—not just as a little kids' storybook or a book for old people preparing to meet their maker. This book is for people of all ages.

As a pastor, father, and grandfather, I have noticed that young kids gravitate to the Scriptures naturally and easily. They love the Bible stories of courage and heroic deeds, such as David taking on Goliath. And they enjoy vivid characters like Jonah and Noah. Children also love to memorize Scripture, since their minds are like sponges, ready and able to soak up everything.

What's more, it is stimulating to have an adult read to them. As a daddy, I know that little boys and girls love to sit alone with Mom or Dad and read. If you are the parent of young ones, you have a tremendous field waiting to be planted. Don't waste their tender years without placing the Scriptures firmly into their hearts. You will not regret it when they become teenagers, believe me. As the Bible says, "Train a child in the way he should go, and when he is old he will not turn from it" (Proverbs 22:6).

The simplicity of learning the Bible is the same for an adult as it is for a child. It is this childlike attitude that heaven encourages. We must become like little children—teachable, enthusiastic, and wide-eyed.

You may say, "Hey, Mike, wait a minute. I am an educated person. I'm not going to act like a kindergartner when learning about the Bible." And in response I say, "The issue is not your level of education; the issue is your approach to learning and your openness to it." That's the beauty of the Bible: God speaks to anyone and everyone who is receptive and eager to hear what He has to say. You may have five doctoral degrees or you may not have made it through the third grade. You may be a speed-reader or you may struggle with dyslexia. You may love to grapple with complex concepts or you may enjoy simple, straightforward truths. Whatever your temperament, background, or education level, God can meet you right where you are.

RELY ON THE HOLY SPIRIT'S INSIGHT

Jesus gave a message one day to His closest friends, telling them that He would soon die and go to heaven. But He promised not leave them alone. He assured them that the Holy Spirit would come and that He would help them understand the things of God.

"I tell you the truth," Jesus said. "It is for your good that I am going away. Unless I go away, the Counselor will not come to you; but if I go, I will send him to you" (John 16:7).

All of this must have raised big questions in the disciples' minds. They must have thought, *Hey, wait a second—what about the kingdom you're going to establish, the one we signed on to help launch? And who's this Counselor you're talking about?* But Jesus knew that these men could handle only so much mind-boggling news at one time:

> *"I have much more to say to you, much more than you can now bear. But when he, the Spirit of truth, comes, he will guide you into all truth. He will not speak on his own; he will speak only what he hears, and he will tell you what is yet to come. He will bring glory to me by taking from what is mine and making it known to you. All that belongs to the Father is mine. That is why I said the Spirit will take from what is mine and make it known to you"* (John 16:12–15).

STUDY THE BIBLE BECAUSE YOU ENJOY LISTENING TO GOD'S SPIRIT OF TRUTH GUIDE YOU INTO ALL TRUTH.

We learn that the Holy Spirit is the Spirit of truth and He will guide us into all truth. That's good news because each of us wants the truth and we all need guidance. Before I became a Christian, I was a seeker of truth, but I could only go so far. My seeking took me to the shores of Japan to read the words of Buddha. I went as far as the Himalayas to learn the words of the gurus and mystics. I explored the occult world to search through bizarre practices and beliefs. But when I found Jesus, I discovered that only He is the way, the truth, and the life.

We are fortunate that God in His infinite wisdom sends us

the Holy Spirit. The Bible eventually ends up in the hands of the people who are seeking God. And the understanding of the Bible eventually makes its way into every seeker's heart and soul, all by the supernatural work of the Holy Spirit. Knowing that the Spirit of God is helping us all along the way, let's look at some steps you can take to get the most out of Bible reading and study:

If You're Not a Scholar, Don't Sweat It

It is true that God made some people to be geniuses—people with big brains and vast understanding. We can thank God for each of them. Though I definitely am not one of them, I appreciate them. All the amazing technology, medical science, and schools of higher education wouldn't exist if brilliant minds hadn't been put to good use.

But the truth is, the majority of us are not geniuses or scholars, and God doesn't expect you to study, think, or act like one. He just wants you to enjoy the Bible and learn to live by it. We do not need to make the Bible so complex that we don't love it. Remember, it is God we love and not pages or concepts or doctrine. It is the Lord Jesus Christ we serve and thank for our salvation. It is the Holy Spirit we learn to trust and who leads us by the Scriptures.

Don't avoid the Scriptures simply because you're not academically inclined or struggle with "book learning." God loves everyone the same—mathematicians and mechanics, CEOs and secretaries, bill collectors and trash collectors. You are unique, and God wants you just the way you are. He is gentle and kind, so be patient with yourself. Whatever you are, wherever you are, He'll speak to you in a manner that you can understand.

Don't Get Caught in "Why-Would-God?" Questions

As a pastor and police chaplain, I have heard over and over again, "Why would a loving God allow this to happen?" or, "Why would God do this to me?" When it comes to the "whys" of God, we often don't know the answer. We don't know everything that God does because He doesn't always check with us and explain Himself.

Our job is not to fully understand God's methods and motivations; our job is to trust Him and have faith in His Word. In fact, God does not expect us to understand what He's doing all the time:

"My thoughts are not your thoughts, neither are your ways my ways," declares the LORD. "As the heavens are higher than the earth, so are my ways higher than your ways and my thoughts than your thoughts. As the rain and the snow come down from heaven, and do not return to it without watering the earth and making it bud and flourish, so that it yields seed for the sower and bread for the eater, so is my word that goes out from my mouth: It will not return to me empty, but will accomplish what I desire and achieve the purpose for which I sent it" (Isaiah 55:8–11).

> LET'S KEEP OUR EYES ON THE MAIN GOAL: TO LOVE GOD WITH OUR HEART, SOUL, AND STRENGTH.

Someday, perhaps, God will reveal everything to us, and it

will all make sense. Until then, we must simply trust that there is a bigger picture than what we see, and we can rest assured that God is in control.

Don't Worry About Things You Don't Understand

In our modern culture, it seems that we need to have an answer for everything. In the spiritual realm, that's not necessary because God has the answer for everything. When you study the Bible, don't stress out when you come upon something that doesn't make sense to you. Just enjoy what you are reading, and hopefully the Holy Spirit will speak to you. As Solomon said, "A wise man will hear and increase learning, and a man of understanding will attain wise counsel" (Proverbs 1:5 NKJV).

It is always a joy to read a portion of Scripture and realize that it speaks to you on a subject you are interested in. The times I enjoy the most are when I am reading stories from the Old Testament that apply directly to my situation. I could be sitting in a room with twenty different people and that same story could have twenty different meanings. But God speaks specifically to me.

Sometimes people start reading the Bible and feel like they are complete wretches. Then they get caught up in seeing only the dark side of things and miss the beauty of God's creation. Let the Bible lift you to heights you have never seen before. Explore the things of the Bible with an open mind and child-like faith. Study to show yourself approved to God, not to man. Study the Bible because you enjoy listening to God's Spirit of truth guiding you into all truth. Don't get stalled by things you come across that puzzle you.

D. L. Moody was one of the most respected and insightful

Bible teachers of the nineteenth century. He wrote many books, founded schools, and preached thousands of times all over the world. He once said, "I am glad there are things in the Bible I do not understand. If I could take that book up and read it as I would any other book, I might begin to think I could write a book like it."[3]

If someone as biblically educated and knowledgeable as Mr. Moody didn't worry about not understanding things in the Bible, neither should we. The Lord knows exactly what He is doing, so dig into the Bible and let Him teach you. Seek after His Word and gain the rewards of a good listener.

Find a Teaching Shepherd

The Bible tells us that God has gifted certain people to teach the Bible: "He Himself gave some to be apostles, some prophets, some evangelists, and some pastors and teachers, for the equipping of the saints for the work of ministry, for the edifying of the body of Christ" (Ephesians 4:11–12 NKJV). Notice that pastor-teachers are a gift from God to equip you for the work of the ministry. Teaching and pastoring are the ministry of the minister. Find a church that teaches the Bible, and find a congregation that has a pastor with a shepherd's heart. As Paul said:

> For as we have many members in one body, but all
> the members do not have the same function, so we,
> being many, are one body in Christ, and individually
> members of one another. Having then gifts differing
> according to the grace that is given to us, let us use
> them: if prophecy, let us prophesy in proportion to our
> faith; or ministry, let us use it in our ministering; he

who teaches, in teaching; he who exhorts, in exhortation; he who gives, with liberality; he who leads, with diligence; he who shows mercy, with cheerfulness (Romans 12:4–8 NKJV).

Look for a church whose leaders demonstrate respect and reverence for God and His Word. Look for a place where you can worship, learn, and grow. Ask the Holy Spirit and He will guide you into "all truth" as you seek the right teacher or pastor to help you deepen your faith.

Find a Good Home Fellowship

When we started our ministry in San Diego in 1974, we began with ten people in a home. Every year since then we have had home fellowships available for the congregation. Why? Because a living-room setting gives people an intimate time in the Bible. It provides a friendly, warm environment in which to ask questions, to talk openly, and to pray with one another.

This is also a training ground for leadership in the church. A pastor must learn to let go and let God lift up people for ministry and leadership roles. It takes trust on the pastor's part to allow others to feed the flock. But a home group allows leaders to practice, gain confidence, and exercise their gifts while being under the oversight of the pastor.

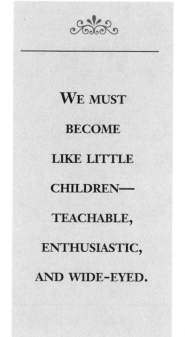

WE MUST BECOME LIKE LITTLE CHILDREN— TEACHABLE, ENTHUSIASTIC, AND WIDE-EYED.

Perhaps you find yourself in an unfamiliar area. Maybe you are in the military or away at college. No matter where you are, gravitate toward a group that is praying and reading the Bible together. This will give you strength throughout the day, knowing that there are other believers nearby.

Don't Become Legalistic

Years ago, Pastor Chuck Smith spoke at our church's school of evangelism. In the class was a young man who made an impressive presentation—he was handsome, muscular, and intellectually bright. He also had a tendency to "split hairs" over the Scriptures and debate every minute detail. The other students knew him as someone who loved to argue about obscure passages and doctrinal details. Frankly, he was a legalist and missed the simplicity of just falling in love with the Bible.

When the class session Chuck taught came to a close, this student immediately approached Chuck and began a scriptural "discussion." I wanted to preserve Chuck's time and to usher him out of the grasp of this "intellectual giant." But Chuck began conversing with him. He softly responded to the questions of the student, as the class gathered around to see the "duel of the century."

The student was taller than Pastor Chuck by about six inches, and Chuck was looking up at this towering hulk of a man. Wisely, Chuck sat down on the floor. This left the man awkwardly arguing with his elder from a distance. Soon, gravity mixed with common sense and this physically imposing student sat on the floor next to Chuck. The two men were now eye-to-eye.

Chuck did the work of an anointed teacher, and to this day his lesson rings in my heart and mind. He gently interrupted the student as he was quoting the Greek and Hebrew and showing off his expansive vocabulary: "Son, remember what Jesus said: 'The Spirit is the Spirit of truth.' He didn't say 'The Spirit is the Spirit of chapter and verse.' In other words, I think it's most important to embrace the spirit of the truth rather than argue over every last issue in the Scripture."

We could go on debating every jot and tittle in the Bible for centuries. Why? What's the point? There will always be someone who wants to debate and argue about the Bible. And there will always be people who will try to convince us that their interpretation is correct. Although we should seek to accurately understand the Bible's intent and we should be clear about our own beliefs, we don't need to get hung up on the "fine print" and endless details. We don't need to "major in the minors."

William Law, a respected theologian and preacher from the eighteenth century, once said:

> *So many intelligent people become preoccupied with dates and linguistic problems in the Bible that they have no time to seriously consider the Bible's main theme, God's love for us and our loving response to Him. They seem so concerned for truth, yet neglect the real purpose of truth, which is to bring us closer to the God of truth.*[4]

Yes, let's keep our eyes on the main goal: to love God with our heart, soul, and strength. When we concentrate on that, we'll not be led down blind alleys and dead-end streets.

One other word of warning: Some people are adamant that a certain translation of the Bible is the only one to use. A segment of Christians believe in *"King James* only." I love the *King*

James Bible, and I have yet to find a translation that is closer to the original Scriptures. However, some people get tripped up by the old-style language— all the *thees* and *thous*. Sometimes it's easier to understand the *Living Bible* or *The Message*, which paraphrase the Scripture into modern language. There are many trustworthy translations you can purchase in a bookstore: the *New American Standard Bible*, the *New International Version*, and the *New King James Version* are all widely accepted and respected.

Ask Your Pastor

An interesting thing happens throughout the world on Sunday mornings. When church services conclude, people line up at the door to shake the hand of their pastor. During these moments, some people look for answers to problems or they request prayer. Personally, I enjoy this because it keeps me aware of the needs in the church. Like most pastors, I find that very few of these encounters concern the Bible. Rarely do people ask questions about the morning message or present issues raised during the week from their Bible reading.

Don't be afraid to ask your pastor about anything and everything. Church leaders are there to serve you and to teach you. The church does not exist for the pastor; the pastor is only a member of the body equipped to feed you God's Word.

Utilize Commentaries and Other Resource Materials

I have a library with many books that help clarify Scripture for me. When I don't understand the meaning of what I am reading, I seek help from a couple of these volumes. It is good to read more than one source so you can learn the different points of view.

Commentaries are written by Bible teachers, scholars, pastors, and others who love to study. These are good for background study, as they teach you things that are not always obvious in the text you are reading. Many times you will learn about the culture and customs that were prevalent during the time of the Bible story.

Hundreds of other books, software, and resources are available to aid and enhance your Bible study. One of my favorites is *Halley's Bible Handbook*, which provides an excellent overview of the Scriptures along with historical and archeological insights.

Devotionals are wonderful tools to have by your side. Not only are there classic devotionals from earlier writers, but you can also find modern writers with topical studies for your daily devotions. A good devotional gives you a biblical text with a short message to stimulate your thinking and provide inspiration. Oswald Chambers' *My Utmost for His Highest* is a classic that has been enjoyed for decades. Another is *Morning and Evening* by Charles Spurgeon, a famous nineteenth-century preacher from London.

Conduct a Word or Character Study

You may benefit from studying a particular word, such as *forgiveness, redemption,* or *giving.* I enjoy doing this, and I apply what I learn to my Bible messages. Often the original word in a text has a much deeper meaning than we perceive when reading it. This deeper meaning can make the difference in application.

I suggest you look in a Christian bookstore for a number of tools that are available. One of the most helpful books is *Strong's Exhaustive Concordance*, which defines every word in the

Bible for you. It has the Hebrew words from the Old Testament and the Greek words from the New Testament. These types of books will help you understand the topics you wish to pursue further.

As you consider how to deepen your understanding of the Scriptures, remember to make prayer a top priority. Without a doubt prayer is the most important and easiest of all ways to understand the Bible. As you read the Scriptures, also pray over them. Ask the Holy Spirit to reveal the truth of the matter to your heart. When you pray, speak to God from your heart.

I included the suggestions in this chapter in hopes that you will fall in love with the Bible. For if you do, you will surely fall in love with God. As I said in an earlier chapter, the Bible is all about growth, progress, and advancement. Your life will keep getting better and better with the help of God and His Word. My friends, I commend the Holy Bible to your lives with the hope that you will fall in love with the message of the Scriptures and fall deeply in love with the God of those Scriptures.

EVERYTHING YOU NEED
IS AT YOUR FINGERTIPS

In chapter 5, I mentioned the film *Cast Away* in which Tom Hanks plays a FedEx executive who gets marooned on a deserted island for many years. During Super Bowl XXXVII, FedEx ran a hilarious commercial that spoofed the movie.

Looking like the scruffy, bedraggled Hanks character, a FedEx employee goes up to the door of a suburban home with a package in hand. When a lady answers the door, he explains that he survived five years on a deserted island, and during that whole time he kept the package safe and unopened in order to deliver it to her.

She replies with a simple, "Thank you."

Naturally, he is curious about what is in the package he protected all those years. He says, "If I may ask, what was in that package after all?"

The woman opens it and shows him the contents, saying, "Oh, nothing really. Just a satellite telephone, a global positioning device, a compass, a water purifier, and some seeds."

All he needed to escape his misery and heartache was there all the time, just waiting to be opened. That's a lot like the Christian life, isn't it? Like the contents in that package, the resources for our freedom, advancement, and victory are available to every Christian who will take advantage of them. They're right there in the Bible, and all we have to do is open it and read it.

As you are about to finish this book, I encourage you to take a moment to pray. Ask the Lord to open your understanding and to give you the ability to learn from the Bible. This is an experience that should change your life forever. The Word of God will fill you with wisdom and discernment. God wants to give you a deeply satisfying spiritual life, and it will come in accordance with your knowledge of His Word. As the apostle Peter said:

TAKE THIS WONDERFUL JOURNEY OF DISCOVERING THE CREATOR OF THE UNIVERSE.

His divine power has given us everything we need for life and godliness through our knowledge of him who called us by his own glory and goodness. Through these he has given us his very great and precious promises, so that through them you may participate in the divine nature and escape the corruption in the world caused by evil desires (2 Peter 1:3–4).

The Bible is indeed filled with great and precious promises. It begins with the proclamation that God created the heavens and the earth. It ends with the words, "The grace of our Lord Jesus Christ be with you all. Amen." In between is everything we could possibly need for a rich, rewarding life.

Take this wonderful journey of discovering the Creator of the universe and the grace of our Lord Jesus Christ, who is coming soon! There will be many distractions and distracters to keep you from the Bible. But let nothing divert you from the power, wisdom, and loving guidance contained in the Scriptures. God is ready to talk with you. Are you listening?

> **GOD WANTS TO GIVE YOU A DEEPLY SATISFYING SPIRITUAL LIFE.**

Your friend,
Mike MacIntosh
San Diego, California

NOTES

Chapter One

1. John Kass, "Waiter's Pen Pal Just a Cool Guy Who Runs a Country," *Chicago Tribune*, July 23, 2001.
2. *Jefferson City News Tribune*, April 25, 2001. This story was retold by Drew Zahn in *Leadership Journal*.

Chapter Two

1. Quoted from CBS news feature "Abuse Scandal Dogs U.S. Catholics." See www.CBSNews.com, January 6, 2004 (CBS/AP).
2. Jeremy Reynalds, "Shamanistic Influences in Korean Pentecostal Christianity: An Analysis," www.rickross.com/reference/yoidoyonggi/yoido1.html.
3. Data from the U.S. Census Bureau Web site: www.census.gov/cgi-bin/ipc/popclockw. January 30, 2004 at 7:55:58 GMT.

Chapter Three

1. Stephen Covey, *Seven Habits of Highly Effective People* (New York: Simon & Schuster, 1989), 24.
2. Ibid., 32.
3. Bill Bright, "Untapped Spiritual Resources," a Campus Crusade publication. www.PreachingToday.com.
4. "Dear Abby" story cited on www.Sermoncentral.com, contributed by Ernest Canell.

Chapter Four

1. Mark Buchanan, *Your God Is Too Safe* (Sisters, Ore.: Multnomah Publishers, 2001), 202.

2. Barna Research Group study results quoted in the *Southeast Outlook*, November 22, 2001. Researchers interviewed 1,004 adults chosen to reflect the United States' regional and ethnic makeup, with a sampling error of plus/minus 3 percent.

3. Robert Coles quoted in *Christianity Today*, February 6, 1987, 20.

4. The Newton Web site Ask a Scientist, sponsored by the Division of Educational Programs at Argonne National Laboratory, http://newton.dep.anl.gov/aasquesv.htm.

5. Tim Quinn, "God, Our Ultimate Troubleshooter," www.PreachingToday.com.

Chapter Five

1. Story cited in an Associated Press article, March 24, 1994, and referenced in *Leadership Journal*, vol. 15, no. 3.

2. Gerald and Geneva Clark, quoted in *Married for Life* (Colorado Springs, Colo.: Honor Books, 2004), 48–49.

3. Laura Pappano, *The Connection Gap: Why Americans Feel So Alone* (New Brunswick, N.J.: Rutgers University Press, 2001), 8.

4. William R. White, *Stories for the Journey* (Grand Rapids, Mich.: Augsburg Press, 1988), 47–49.

Chapter Six

1. Daniel Taylor, *Tell Me a Story* (St. Paul, Minn.: Bog Walk Press, 2001)

2. Frederick Buechner, *Telling the Truth* (San Francisco: HarperSanFrancisco, 1985), 23.

3. Kurt Bruner, *The Divine Drama* (Wheaton, Ill.: Tyndale House, 2001), 19, 22.

4. Cited in Timothy George, "Big Picture Faith," Christianity Today, October 23, 2000. Vol. 44, no.12, p. 88.

Chapter Eight

1. John MacArthur, *The Freedom and Power of Forgiveness*, (Wheaton, Ill.: Crossway Books, 1998)

2. Frederick C. Grant, quoted on WorldofQuotes.com www.worldofquotes.com/topic/Christianity/7/.

3. Jill Lieber, "Teen Surfer Riding Wave of Amazing Grace," *USA Today*, March 19, 2004.

Chapter Nine

1. Elisabeth Elliot, "The Liberty of Obedience," *Christianity Today*, April 8, 1985. Vol. 31, no. 14.

2. Haddon Robinson, "The Wisdom of Small Creatures," www.PreachingToday.com.

Chapter Ten

1. George Barna, *What Americans Believe* (Ventura, Calif.: Regal Books, 2001), 31.

2. Ibid., 285–286.

3. D. L. Moody quoted in *Christian History*, vol. 5, no. 25.

4. William Law, "Christian Perfection," *Christianity Today*, March 30, 1987. Vol. 33, no. 13, paraphrased by Marvin D. Hinten.

READERS' GUIDE

*FOR PERSONAL REFLECTION
OR GROUP DISCUSSION*

FALLING IN LOVE WITH THE BIBLE

The great evangelist Billy Graham once said, "Don't be afraid to invest in the best Bible you can afford—for that is what you are making: an investment. Find out for yourself why it answers every human need, why it supplies the faith and strength that keeps humanity marching forward."

The statement echoes one of the themes woven throughout this book: Reading the Bible and studying consistently is an investment that reaps huge dividends. Doing so will enrich your personal life, enhance your relationships, and enable you to find purpose and meaning. Most of all, diligent Bible reading allows you to become better acquainted with its Author, the heavenly Father who greatly desires to speak with you through the pages of His book. The apostle Paul captures well our aim:

> *I keep asking that the God of our Lord Jesus Christ,*
> *the glorious Father, may give you the Spirit of wisdom and*
> *revelation, so that you may know him better. I pray also*
> *that the eyes of your heart may be enlightened in order that*
> *you may know the hope to which he has called you, the*

*riches of his glorious inheritance in the saints, and his
incomparably great power (Ephesians 1:17–19).*

That is the ultimate goal of falling in love with the Bible—
to know God better and share in the blessings promised to
those who walk closely with Him. The following study—indeed
this entire book—is intended to inspire and invigorate your
Bible reading so that the power of God may revolutionize every
aspect of your existence.

The questions that follow have been designed for use by
individuals or groups. Use this guide during your personal
devotions, with a prayer partner, in a study group, or in a
Sunday school class. However you utilize this study, may you
gain a deeper appreciation for the gift of God's Word.

CHAPTER ONE: COMMUNICATING WITH THE CREATOR

1. The idea underlying everything in this book can be
   summed up in this sentence: "When you fall in love with
   the Bible, you'll fall in love with God." Why do you think
   reading and studying the Bible is so important for cultivat-
   ing a love relationship with God?

2. The writer of Hebrews says that the Bible is "living and
   active" (4:12). What do you think this means? How can a
   book—made of paper, ink, and binding—be alive? Do you
   experience the Word of God as living and active in your
   life? In what ways could it be even more so?

3. It is true, as Mike says in this chapter, that God reveals
   Himself to us through the Bible. What in particular have
   you learned about God's character recently as you've read
   the Scriptures? What aspect of God do you hope to learn
   more about in the coming weeks and months?

4. Mike says, "We can approach the Bible not as a dry manuscript or history text, but as a way to develop closeness

with our Father." How does God use His book to foster closeness with us? Can you recall a time when reading the Bible left you feeling particularly close to God? Why was the experience especially meaningful for you?

5. This chapter contains a quotation from theologian A. W. Tozer: "God is not silent. It is the nature of God to speak. … The Bible is the inevitable outcome of God's continuous speech. It is the infallible declaration of His mind." Besides the Bible, in what other ways does God speak to you and reveal Himself? Do you find it easy or difficult to hear God speaking to you through the Bible? How can you better listen for God's voice while reading His book?

CHAPTER TWO: TAKE ANOTHER LOOK AT THE BOOK

1. Mike asserts that the society in which we live largely presents a negative view of the Bible. Do you agree? Can you think of a specific example of how our culture (the media, universities, and so on) tries to discredit and demean the Bible?

2. Mike confesses that when he was young, he considered the Bible to be a "book for old people." What was your view of the Bible as a young person? In what ways did your family and community shape your perception of Scripture? How has your perception of the Bible changed over the years?

3. This chapter presents several reasons why people sometimes have a distorted view of the Bible, including painful childhood experiences, the myth that it is only a book of "dos and don'ts," false cultural and societal impressions, and the notion that it is outdated and irrelevant. Which of these factors is most prevalent among people you know who avoid the Bible? Can you add to this list of reasons people steer clear of the Bible?

4. Centuries ago, the apostle Paul wrote, "The god of this age has blinded the minds of unbelievers, so that they cannot see the light of the gospel of the glory of Christ." What was true then seems to be true today as well. Paul goes on to say, "For God, who said, 'Let light shine out of darkness,' made his light shine in our hearts to give us the light of the knowledge of the glory of God" (2 Corinthians 4:4, 6). How has God worked in your life to make "His light shine" in your heart? In what ways can you "shine out in darkness" so others can see the truth of God's Word?

5. Since God is eager to speak with His children through the pages of His book, what specifically prevents you from reading the Bible more often?

CHAPTER THREE: THE PARADIGM OF PRIVILEGE

1. In this chapter, Mike makes the point that Bible reading is a "get to," not a "have to." Why do so many people, Christians included, see it as a "have to"? Do you approach the Bible as a "get to," with eagerness and anticipation? If not, why is that?

2. This chapter quotes business expert Stephen Covey: "Paradigms are powerful because they create the lens through which we see the world." What was the paradigm you grew up with in regard to the Bible, church, and spiritual matters? In what way, if any, does your paradigm toward the Bible need to shift to become more positive?

3. Mike paraphrased a quote by Abraham Lincoln to say, "People get out of the Bible about as much as they choose

to." What does that mean to you exactly? Do you agree with that statement? How can you get more out of the Bible in the coming weeks and months?

4. Psalm 19 says, "The statutes of the LORD are right, rejoicing the heart; the commandment of the LORD is pure, enlightening the eyes" (v. 8 NKJV). Have you read anything in the Bible recently that caused your heart to rejoice? Have you read anything that enlightened you or opened your eyes to a new truth or insight?

5. This chapter ends with a story of when Mike and his boyhood pal, Dewey, sought counsel from Dewey's grandparents. The encounter made a great impression on Mike, especially because of the older couple's obvious love for God and the Bible. Do you know someone whose love for the Scriptures impresses you? Is there someone in your life you look to as a role model in matters of faith and the Christian life? What exactly makes this individual so admirable to you?

CHAPTER FOUR: CHECK THE DIRECTIONS

1. Mike suggests the Bible is like an "owner's manual," providing guidance and wisdom for any issue we might encounter. In what ways has the Bible offered specific help to you in the past? What problems or issues are you currently facing that might be resolved with the help of God's Word?

2. The psalmist asked, "How can a young man cleanse his way? By taking heed according to Your word" (119:9 NKJV). And a New Testament passage says we can be cleansed "by the washing with water through the word" (see Ephesians 5:25–26). What do you think it means to be cleansed by the Word? How do we become clean through this process?

3. Our human pride sometimes keeps us from seeking counsel from God's Word. We think we can handle everything on our own. What else might cause people to look somewhere besides the Bible for help and guidance in times of trouble? Where do you tend to go first when you're dealing with a problem?

4. In this chapter, Mike shares one of his favorite psalms: "How precious also are thy thoughts unto me, O God! How great is the sum of them! If I should count them, they are more in number than the sand" (139:17–18 KJV). How do you respond to knowing that God thinks so highly—and so often—of you? How does this passage affect your sense of significance?

5. In the section called "The Bible Is Your Guide to Adventure," Mike writes, "I don't want to live a predictable, humdrum life. I want to participate in God's outrageous plan to love, help, and rescue people all over the world." Assuming you share these sentiments, how can the Bible help you live more adventurously? What can you do in the coming year to participate more fully and actively in God's plan for the world?

CHAPTER FIVE: YOU ARE NOT ALONE

1. The book of Acts describes the early community of believers as "one in heart and mind" (see Acts 4). What specifically promotes unity among believers? What erodes it? How could Christians in general, or smaller groups of believers in specific, enjoy more oneness in heart and mind today?

2. Mike says that "loneliness may be the single greatest cause of emotional, physical, and spiritual maladies in our society." Do you agree? If so, what can you do to help alleviate loneliness in your own life and in the lives of others?

3. The Bible emphasizes the value of being part of a close fellowship of believers. How important is it to you to participate in a community? Why is it so difficult to develop a sense of belonging and community in our society?

4. The Scriptures contain stories and specific guidance for virtually every kind of relationship: marriages, friendships, neighbors, fellow believers, bosses and employees, parents and children, and so on. What relationship in your life would you like to improve? How can you utilize the Bible to accomplish this?

5. This chapter features a quote from the renowned evangelist and educator D. L. Moody: "The Bible was not given to increase our knowledge but to change our lives." In what specific area would you like God, through His Word, to change your life?

CHAPTER SIX: WHAT'S YOUR STORY?

1. What is one of your favorite stories in the Bible? Why does this story resonate with you? What have you learned from the story that applies to your life?

2. Mike says the Bible is really a "story that began at Creation, continues today, and will keep on spreading out into the future. The point is that you are contributing to the story that unfolds and unfurls like a ribbon in time." Do you have a sense of connection to the past and the future? How does the notion that you are part of "God's unfolding drama" change the way you view your everyday life?

3. This chapter features a quotation from Daniel Taylor: "Stories tell us who we are, why we are here, and what we are to do. They give us our best answers to all of life's big questions, and to most of the small ones as well." Why are stories such powerful teaching tools? Why do you think God chose to instruct us through so many vivid biblical stories, and why did Jesus include so many stories in His teaching?

4. Mike told about two of his favorite biblical characters, Elijah and Jeremiah, and shared what he learned from their stories. He says, "I encourage you to choose your own favorite characters—people you can identify with—and learn as much as you can from them." Is there a character in the Bible you are drawn to? Why is this? What can you do to learn from this person's experiences?

5. God does not call any of us to be famous, popular, or prominent. In fact, Jesus said, "If anyone wants to be first, he must be the very least—the servant of all." And, "For he who is least among you all—he is the greatest" (Mark 9:35; Luke 9:48). In what ways does this instruction run counter to society's prevailing beliefs? Why do some people think they have to be a superstar in order to make a difference for God? What does it mean in our day and age to be "the servant of all"?

CHAPTER SEVEN: FORTIFY YOUR FAITH

1. Oswald Chambers wrote: "Living a life of faith means never knowing where you are being led. But it does mean loving and knowing the One who is leading." Have you had an experience in which you were forced to trust God's leading even when you couldn't see the road ahead? How did you handle that situation? How did it affect your faith?

2. In what aspect of life do you find it most difficult to live by faith? How can you utilize the Bible to help you bolster your faith in this area?

3. The writer of Hebrews tells us, "Now faith is the substance of things hoped for, the evidence of things not seen" (11:1 KJV). What do you think that means? How does it apply to your daily life?

4. Another passage in Hebrews says, "But without faith it is impossible to please God." Why is faith so important to God? Do you think this means the more faith someone has, the more pleasing he or she is to God?

5. In this chapter, Mike says, "Like our relationships with our loved ones, our relationship with God should never be stagnant; we must always strive to continue growing in faith." What are some specific ways you can keep your relationship with God growing and vibrant?

CHAPTER EIGHT: ADVERSITY IS AN ALLY

1. It's safe to say that no one welcomes hardship and heartache, but they are an inevitable part of life. How can you turn difficulties into opportunities to grow? What can you learn from the Bible to shift your perspective about adversity?

2. In this chapter, Mike says, "Like our forebears in the faith, we can be a testimony to those around us by demonstrating grace in the midst of problems and peril." Can you think of someone you know whose faith and courage in a time of trouble inspired you? Have you had a chance to demonstrate grace in the midst of hardship?

3. Which biblical character speaks to you most clearly about courage amid crisis or perseverance amid peril? What can you learn from this person that applies to your own life?

4. "[The Lord] said to me, 'My grace is sufficient for you, for my power is made perfect in weakness.' … For when I am weak, then I am strong" (2 Corinthians 12:9–10). What did Paul mean by, "My power is made perfect in weakness"? And why did he say that when he's weak, he is strong?

5. Paul also wrote to his protégé, Timothy, "For God has not given us a spirit of fear, but of power and of love and of a sound mind" (2 Timothy 1:7 NKJV). How might those three elements—power, love, and a sound mind—complement each other in the midst of a fearful situation? How can we replace the fear we feel with power, love, and a sound mind?

CHAPTER NINE: GETTING BETTER ALL THE TIME

1. Mike says, "The Bible is a book of momentum and forward progress. There are literally hundreds of references to words such as *continue, progress, mature, grow, increase,* and *carry on.*" What sometimes hinders people from progressing? Besides Bible reading, what ways can you promote growth in your life?

2. God put each person on earth for a reason—with a mission to accomplish. As the psalmist wrote, "The LORD will fulfill his purpose for me" (138:8). Do you have a clear sense of your purpose? If not, how can you become clearer about it? How can the Bible help you in this endeavor?

3. What causes some Christians to be fired up about their faith while others are burned out? What is it that makes the difference between a "true, passionate Christian" and a "Christian church attendee"?

4. Many men and women start out their Christian life with enthusiasm and dedication but eventually fade away. As Mike says, "Because the Christian life demands so much of us—because growth is usually a process of 'two steps forward, one step back'—many people give up." Why exactly do some people abandon the faith or become stagnant? How can you ensure that your faith stays strong over the long haul?

5. The writer of Hebrews says, "Though by this time you ought to be teachers, you need someone to teach you the elementary truths of God's word all over again. You need milk, not solid food!" (5:12). What are some ways to make sure you don't stay stuck at the "elementary truths" stage? How can you move beyond milk and on to solid food? How can you encourage others to do the same?

CHAPTER TEN: MINING FOR GOLD

1. Thankfully, we are not left on our own to try to understand the Bible. Jesus promised that when He went away, He would send a Counselor: "When he, the Spirit of truth, comes, he will guide you into all truth" (John 16:13). How can we tap into the power of the Holy Spirit to guide us into truth? How can we know if the Holy Spirit is helping us or not?

2. This chapter makes clear that God, through His Word, meets us wherever we are. We might be rich or poor, educated or uneducated, a brand-new Christian or veteran of the faith—it doesn't matter. The Bible speaks to everyone. In what way does God speak to you through His book? Can you think of two people who are vastly different and yet both learn much from the Bible? How does God accomplish this?

3. Mike cautions against debating every fine point, every jot and tittle, in the Bible. That's because some people get bogged down by focusing on the minutiae and miss the big picture. What's the balance between seeking to know what you believe and merely debating endlessly? How can you turn a fruitless debate into a productive discussion?

4. Jesus told His disciples, "Assuredly, I say to you, unless you are converted and become as little children, you will by no means enter the kingdom of heaven" (Matthew 18:3 NKJV). What did He mean? How can we "become as little children"?

5. This chapter presents several practical suggestions to help you enjoy the Bible and understand it better. What new ideas might you incorporate to deepen your appreciation of Scripture and broaden your knowledge of it? How can you ensure that your understanding of the Bible continues to expand year after year?

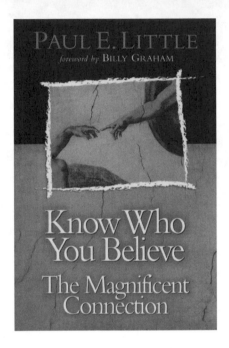
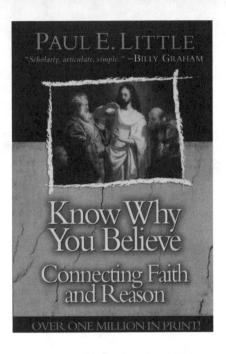

The Word at Work Around the World

A vital part of Cook Communications Ministries is our international outreach, Cook Communications Ministries International (CCMI). Your purchase of this book, and of other books and Christian-growth products from Cook, enables CCMI to provide Bibles and Christian literature to people in more than 150 languages in 65 countries.

Cook Communications Ministries is a not-for-profit, self-supporting organization. Revenues from sales of our books, Bible curricula, and other church and home products not only fund our U.S. ministry, but also fund our CCMI ministry around the world. One hundred percent of donations to CCMI go to our international literature programs.

CCMI reaches out internationally in three ways:

· Our premier International Christian Publishing Institute (ICPI) trains leaders from nationally led publishing houses around the world.

· We provide literature for pastors, evangelists, and Christian workers in their national language.

· We reach people at risk—refugees, AIDS victims, street children, and famine victims—with God's Word.

Word Power, God's Power

Faith Kidz, RiverOak, Honor, Life Journey, Victor, NexGen — every time you purchase a book produced by Cook Communications Ministries, you not only meet a vital personal need in your life or in the life of someone you love, but you're also a part of ministering to José in Colombia, Humberto in Chile, Gousa in India, or Lidiane in Brazil. You help make it possible for a pastor in China, a child in Peru, or a mother in West Africa to enjoy a life-changing book. And because you helped, children and adults around the world are learning God's Word and walking in his ways.

Thank you for your partnership in helping to disciple the world. May God bless you with the power of his Word in your life.

For more information about our international ministries, visit www.ccmi.org.

Additional copies of *FALLING IN LOVE WITH THE BIBLE*
and other Victor titles are available
from your local bookseller.

If you have enjoyed this book,
or if it has had an impact on your life,
we would like to hear from you.

Please contact us at:

VICTOR BOOKS
Cook Communications Ministries, Dept. 201
4050 Lee Vance View
Colorado Springs, CO 80918
Or visit our Web site: www.cookministries.com

For our European readers:
KINGSWAY COMMUNICATIONS LTD
Lottbridge Drove, Eastbourne BN23 6NT, England
E-mail: books@kingsway.co.uk

The Bible Teacher's Teacher